CUB0919111

Guide 96

Pavel Kholkov in the title role in 1881. He created the role in the professional première at the Bolshoi, Moscow on January 23, 1881. (Royal Opera House Archives)

Preface

This series, published under the auspices of English National Opera and The Royal Opera, aims to prepare audiences to evaluate and enjoy opera in performance. Each book contains the complete text, set out in this case in transliteration, beside a modern English performing translation. The introductory essays, illsustrations and musical analysis have been chosen to focus attention on some of the points of special interest in each work. We hope that, as companions to the opera should be, they are well-informed, witty and attractive.

The Royal Opera is most grateful to The Baring Foundation for sponsoring this Guide.

Nicholas John
Series Editor

38

Eugene Onegin

Pyotr Tchaikovsky

Opera Guide Series Editor: Nicholas John

Published in association with
English National Opera and The Royal Opera
and assisted by a generous donation from The Baring Foundation

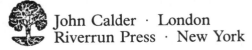

John Calder · London
Riverrun Press · New York

First published in Great Britain, 1988 by
John Calder (Publishers) Ltd.,
18 Brewer Street,
London, W1R 4AS

First published in the U.S.A., 1988 by
Riverrun Press Inc.,
1170 Broadway,
New York, NY 10001

BRITISH LIBRARY CATALOGUING IN PUBLICATION DATA

Chaikovskii, P.I. (Peter Ilich), *1840-1893*
    Eugene Onegin.—(Opera guide 38)
    1. Opera in Russian. Chaikovskii, P.I.
    (Peter Ilich) 1840-1893. Eugenii Onegin
    I. Title   II. English National Opera
    III. Royal Opera   IV. Series   V. Eugenii
    Onegin; Libretto. *English and Russian*
    782.1'092'4

    ISBN 0-7145-4146-X

LIBRARY OF CONGRESS CATALOG NUMBER

88-060603

Typeset in Plantin by Maggie Spooner Typesetting, London
Printed by The Camelot Press Ltd., Southampton.

Contents

List of Illustrations

Picture research: Henrietta Bredin

Pushkin into Tchaikovsky:
Caustic Novel, Sentimental Opera

Caryl Emerson

It is a paradox of Russian culture that Alexander Pushkin (1799-1837), that restlessly ironic poet and master of the subtle and swiftly-moving scene, should have proved so popular a source for opera. For the nineteenth-century opera libretto tended to heroicize, slow things down, replace narrative irony with fully-committed dramatic aria. Conciseness and emotional constraint, those great trademarks of Pushkin's mature style, transpose poorly into music drama. In fact, almost everything that Pushkin parodied about Romanticism was, loosely speaking, 'operatic'.

But happily, musical adaptations are not to be judged solely by criteria of fidelity. A great variety of relationships, ingenious and multi-voiced, are possible between a libretto and its source text. The complexities here in fact resemble those we confront when evaluating translations from one national language into another: interlinear cribs succeed on one level and satisfy one purpose, whereas 'poetic imitations' are assessed according to other criteria and satisfy us in a different way. The equivalent processes in songwriting and opera would be (on the one hand) literal word-for-word settings that aim to 'realize' the verbal text, and (on the other hand) free adaptations that in effect discard the text once a basic cast of characters and some blunt plots have been extracted. Tchaikovsky's version of Pushkin's *Eugene Onegin* belongs to a third and intermediate category, however, in many ways the most theoretically challenging.

This last category of opera is organized around the principle of 'scenes from classic works'. The opera composer follows the source text closely in some areas and violates it appallingly in others. But these departures from the text are not, strictly speaking, infidelities, because the audience of a 'scenes-from' opera is expected to know the *from*. The libretto is not obliged to retell the story; what happens on stage is not new information but rather a reminder of something already intimately known. Such libretti thus presume the sort of audience implied for epic performances. The story is familiar — and thus suspense, sequence of events, and the specifics of start and finish are not at issue. Such cultural knowledge is part of any performance of a 'scenes-from' opera, where the audience does not expect a full text any more than a reader, familiar with a novel, would expect its illustrations alone to 'tell the whole story'. The success and appeal of the transposition lie precisely in the variation of a known text under new circumstances.

Pushkin's *Eugene Onegin* — the masterpiece of the nation's master poet — had achieved that status in Russian culture by 1877. In that year Tchaikovsky, after some hesitation, decided to take on the challenge of an operatic setting. Since that time, lovers of Pushkin have repeatedly maligned the composer and his librettist brother Modeste for 'destroying' and 'violating' Pushkin's original. Yet a derived text need not, of course, be perceived as a threat or a distortion. Pushkin is put in no danger by the existence of sentimental libretti drawing on his characters and occasionally on his verse. In fact, it could even be argued that Tchaikovsky, far from misreading Pushkin's original, intended his composition to say something about the *in*compatibility of opera and

Ileana Cotrubas as Tatyana and Thomas Allen as Onegin in the production by Peter Hall, designed by Julia Trevelyan Oman at Covent Garden in 1986 (photo: Clive Barda)

novel. In an oft-cited letter to Sergei Taneev (January 1878), the composer made his fears and intentions clear:

> I composed this opera because I was moved to express in music all that seems to cry out for such expression in *Eugene Onegin* . . . The opera *Onegin* will never have a success [at the major houses]: I already feel assured of that . . . I would much prefer to confide it to the theatre of the Conservatoire . . . This is much more suitable to my modest work, which I shall not describe as an opera, if it is published. I should like to call it 'lyrical scenes' or something of that kind.[1]

Tchaikovsky did in fact subtitle his *Onegin* 'lyrical scenes', which suggests not a musical realization or embodiment of Pushkin but something much bolder: selected portions of Pushkin's novel reworked in the lyric mode. Pushkin's poetic gift was dry, ironic, often cruel on characters and on readers. Tchaikovsky's musical gift — by his own insistent testimony — was almost entirely emotional and sentimental. The very existence of this opera alongside its source text serves to reconfirm the uniqueness of Pushkin's novel rather than to undermine it.

What sort of work, then, is Pushkin's original? Like *Boris Godunov*, the other great operaticized Pushkin classic, *Eugene Onegin* has become for Western audiences a story that has always been sung. But unlike Pushkin's dramatic chronicle *Boris* — which never really succeeded on the stage, and which many would say has gained in stature through its operatic setting — Pushkin's *Onegin* was celebrated from the start as an untranslatable miracle of form. Written and published during the years 1824-1829, *Eugene Onegin* is a 'novel in verse' of some five and a half thousand lines. It is set for the most part in intricately rhyming fourteen-line stanzas distributed over eight chapters or cantos. On the level of plot, the tale is banal — if not outright repulsive. Eugene Onegin, a young Petersburg fop (or 'drawing-room automaton', as Nabokov calls him), wearies of city life and retires to his recently inherited country estate (Chapter One). There he makes friends with Vladimir Lensky, a young and very romantic poet on a neighbouring estate, and together the two plan to call at the home of Lensky's betrothed, Olga Larina (Chapter Two). The visit takes place. As Lensky sings the praises of his bride, Olga's older sister Tatyana falls instantly and irreversibly in love with the aloof Onegin. She writes him a letter (in 79 moving, freely-rhymed lines) declaring her love; Onegin does not respond (Chapter Three). Finally he pays a visit to reprimand Tatyana, correctly but condescendingly, for her presumptuous act, adding that he was not made for conjugal bliss (Chapter Four). Tatyana is mortified, and in a terrifying erotic dream imagines herself pursued through snowdrifts by a shaggy bear and ultimately entertained at table by monsters whose master is Onegin. Soon after, Tatyana celebrates her nameday. Both Onegin and Lensky attend, and Onegin, giving vent to his playful spleen, teases Lensky by flirting with Olga. Lensky leaves the Larins in a jealous fury (Chapter Five). The following day Lensky challenges Onegin to a duel. Onegin agrees indifferently, and kills his friend on the first shot (Chapter Six). Some time passes. Olga quickly marries another, Onegin leaves for foreign lands, and Tatyana (still smitten) visits Onegin's abandoned house, seeking in his library some clue to his strange character. Madame Larina, worried about her elder daughter, takes her to the Moscow 'marriage market' (Chapter

1. See Modeste Tchaikovsky, *The Life and Letters of Peter Ilich Tchaikovsky*, ed. and trans. Rosa Newmarch (New York: John Lane, 1906), pp. 255-7.

M. Klimentova as Tatyana in the performance of extracts from the opera at the Moscow Conservatory in 1878. She created the role in the following year.

Seven). Several more years pass. Onegin returns to St Petersburg and happens to meet Tatyana at a ball; she has become a sophisticated, well-disciplined society belle, and is married to an elderly general. It is now Onegin's turn to fall immediately and irreversibly in love. But his requests for an interview (and his passionate letter) all remain unanswered. Only when he arrives at Tatyana's residence unannounced and falls at her feet does she sternly declare that 'she loves him still, but has been given to another, to whom she will remain forever faithful.' With his unfortunate hero in that symmetrically satisfying position, Pushkin takes leave of his novel (Chapter Eight).

Two points must be emphasized about this plot. First, it is told by a witty, aggressive narrator, who only partly speaks for Pushkin, and who weaves into it lengthy digressions, sly ruminations and commentary that in fact constitute the genius of this otherwise undistinguished tale. Secondly, and in apparent contradiction to the above point, the critical reception of *Onegin* in the nineteenth century tended to strip away precisely what was extraordinary about the work — this inventive and provocative narrative voice.[2] In the 1840s

2. For a good anthology in English of the relevant essays, see Sona Hoisington, ed. and trans., *Russian Views of Pushkin's 'Eugene Onegin'* (Bloomington: Indiana University Press, 1988).

A. Nejdanova as Tatyana at the Bolshoi in 1906.

Vissarion Belinsky, 'father' of Russian literary criticism, wrote of Onegin and Tatyana as if they were real-life social types, and burdened their relationship with the suffering and sociopolitical impotence expected of educated subjects of the Russian Empire. The radical critic Dmitri Pisarev, writing on the work in the 1860s, railed equally and on the same plane against the author Pushkin, his hero Eugene Onegin, *and* the critic Belinsky — the first two for their aristocratic enthusiasms and Byronic *ennui*, and Belinsky for being taken in by them, that is, for blaming the moral flaws of the Pushkins and the Onegins on society and not on the men themselves. Pisarev did not even touch upon questions of irony, narrative voice, or the fact that the novel was a fiction. By the time Fyodor Dostoevsky delivered his famous 'Pushkin Speech' at the unveiling of the Pushkin Monument in Moscow (1880), there was ample precedent for misinterpreting the tonality of *Eugene Onegin* at almost every crucial point. In that speech, Dostoevsky invested Tatyana's decision not to leave her elderly husband for Onegin with all the moral and millenarian pathos of Ivan Karamazov's challenge to God. 'Can anyone', Dostoevsky wrote of the heroine, 'possibly build his happiness on the unhappiness of another?'

Through such readings, Pushkin, an enlightened conservative with profound sympathy for his own beleaguered class, was being successfully reinvented as a left-wing radical in one decade and a right-wing nationalist in another. This history of critical reception should be kept firmly in mind when considering the musical and literary contexts for Tchaikovsky's 1878 operatic interpretation of *Eugene Onegin*. By that time, Pushkin's plot from the 1820s had long since entered the public domain. It was being read through literary and social events of the second half of the century.

Soviet music historians have in fact suggested two different lines along which Tchaikovsky transposed Pushkin's texts into opera.[3] The first might be called the 'Dostoevsky line', marked by large, tragic gestures culminating in violence or madness. The central texts here are Pushkin's *Bronze Horseman* and *Queen of Spades*, and the relevant Dostoevskian filter is, of course, Raskolnikov. Hermann, the hero of Tchaikovsky's *Queen of Spades*, does indeed resemble the hero of *Crime and Punishment* in that he, too, cannot be satisfied with mere disillusionment, with *ennui* pure and simple. The cold calculations of the 'superfluous man' in Pushkin's tale give way to emotionally extravagant acts of murder or suicide. The other tendency, much more restrained, could be called the 'Turgenev line'. Here, as in Turgenev's novels and dramas, we confront a vocabulary of small gestures, domesticity, and patient longing. Whatever crises do erupt are resolved by the strength and self-discipline of women. Clearly, Tchaikovsky's master text in this line is his *Eugene Onegin*.

Let us consider several aspects of the opera from this point of view. Libretti leave out a great deal, and it should not surprise us that much of Pushkin's novel is lost — most importantly, the rhythmic pace of that severely uniform 'Onegin stanza' which sheathed a garrulous narrator and a world of warring intonations. But on closer inspection it is quite remarkable how much has been left in. Whole chunks of Pushkin's verse are set almost unchanged: Tatyana's letter to Onegin (Act One, Scene Two), for example; Onegin's response (Act One, Scene Three); and Lensky's farewell verses in Act Two, Scene Two (although they are transposed to the scene of the duel). Occasionally the characters sing to others what Pushkin has them only think. The famous opening stanza of the novel, which Onegin speaks to himself en route to his dying uncle, is sung to Tatyana in the opera at the end of their first meeting (Act One, Scene One).

Still other passages are recast from the narrator's sphere into the mouths of the heroes, imparting to these characters a strangely naive immediacy. Onegin, for example, sings at the nameday party of his dissatisfaction with his own irresponsible behaviour in ensemble with the insulted Lensky (Act Two, Scene One), and in the following scene — right before the fatal shot is fired — Lensky and Onegin sing a duet drawn from the *narrator's* rhetorical plea for reconciliation. To be sure, such operatic juxtapositions and externalizations of the inner self are perhaps inevitable compensation for the absence of a narrator, and exploit (quite properly) what music does best. Tchaikovsky goes further, however, subtly re-accenting his characters' lines so that all genuinely conditional and ambivalent elements are removed. In a famous piece of advice

3. Boris Asafiev and Abram Gozenpud have both advanced such theses. See the discussion in B. Ya. Anshakov, 'O nekotorykh chertakh khudozhestvennogo mira P.I. Chaikovskogo i osobennostiakh pereomysleniia pushkinskikh obrazakh v opere *Pikovaia dama*,' in *P.I. Chaikovskii i russkaia literatura* (Izhevsk, 'Udmurtiia', 1980), pp. 125-28.

Amy Shuard as Tatyana at Sadler's Wells in 1952 (photo: Angus McBean © Harvard Theatre Collection)

to Lensky in the novel (Chapter Three, v), Onegin, considering the two Larin sisters, remarks: 'I would have chosen the other one if I were, like you, a poet.' But the whole novel rests on the fact that Onegin is *not* a poet. In fact, he creates and imagines nothing, and is almost completely defined by what he negates, by what he has ceased to care about.[4] Negation is notoriously difficult to transmit musically, and Tchaikovsky, weaving that line into a quartet between the four principals (Act One, Scene One), has Onegin repeat only the first and more affirmative half of the phrase at the end of the number.

In the final category of text — unmistakably marked in Russian, for the poetry is doggerel — there are those lines completely invented by Tchaikovsky in collaboration with his two fellow librettists (his brother Modeste and the minor poet K.S. Shilovsky). Exemplary here are Lensky's love transports and Gremin's famous aria. The effect of these amateur interpolations into a scene dominated by chunks of Pushkin's text is most peculiar on the Russian ear that knows Pushkin's *Onegin* by heart. They tend to make the whole ironic, and bring, as it were, two quite separate universes into contact. But as Tchaikovsky said of his later opera *The Queen of Spades*, he stood by the scene and not by the word.[5] What, for him, were the crucial scenes?

The answer is easy enough: those scenes where Tatyana is central, and particularly where she is in a state of painful longing.[6] The entire opera is in fact told from her point of view, with her reactions to the world given primary expression. Tchaikovsky did not much like Onegin. Significantly, the opera opens not on the hero's dissolute life in Petersburg but directly on material from Chapter Two: the two Larin daughters and their mother, singing of the blessedness of habit and fidelity. Ambivalent or erotic elements, such as Tatyana's dream, are passed over in silence. In his work on the opera, Tchaikovsky appears to have progressively 'cleansed' his heroine. In the first version of the libretto, the ending was considerably more painful and passionate for both parties: Tatyana struggled with her conscience over many pages, even allowing herself to fall into Onegin's arms — and when she finally found the courage to dismiss her suitor, he cried out for death to release him. Ultimately, however, Onegin was reduced to repeating his declaration of love to a stern audience, and his passion is in no way ennobled.[7] A recent reading of the final scene[8] even suggests that Tchaikovsky intended us to perceive Onegin's desperate courtship of Tatyana *ironically* — since the composer sets

4. See J. Douglas Clayton, *Ice and Flame: Aleksandr Pushkin's 'Eugene Onegin'* (Toronto: University of Toronto Press, 1985), ch. 5.

5. From Tchaikovsky's letter to his brother Modeste, February 20, 1890. See the good discussion of this, and other particulars of Tchaikovsky's libretto aesthetic, in E.M. Orlova, *Petr Il'ich Chaikovskii* (Moscow: Muzyka, 1980), pp. 171-81.

6. For more on the nature of Tchaikovsky's borrowings from Pushkin, see Gerald Abraham, *The Music of Tchaikovsky* (New York: Norton, 1974), pp. 147-54; and Gary Schmidgall, *Literature as Opera* (New York: Oxford University Press, 1977), ch. 7.

7. The Lloyd-Jones translation included in this volume appears to favour some version of Tchaikovsky's initial variant ('Now only death remains!'). The Russian text of the definitive version of Onegin's final lines (for the Bolshoi Theatre première in 1881) reads instead 'Disgrace! Anguish! How pitiable is my fate!' This is the line usually sung on Soviet recordings of the opera, and is much more in keeping with the spirit of Pushkin's own desperate (but not melodramatic) conclusion.

8. Nicholas G. Žekulin (University of Calgary), '*Evgenii Onegin*: Novel to Opera. The Art of Adaptation', paper delivered at Pushkin Symposium, University of Ottawa, February 26-28, 1987.

Giuseppe De Luca as Onegin and Claudia Muzio as Tatyana at the Metropolitan Opera, New York in 1921 (photo: Metropolitan Opera Archives)

this frantic wooing to orchestral themes and textures first heard in Onegin's rejection of Tatyana in Act One, Scene Three. Tatyana knows that Onegin has not changed, that his themes are thin, and the presence of Lensky's themes throughout the final act continually reminds us of that act of indifferent violence. Indeed, Tchaikovsky had little faith in Onegin. As in Turgenev's novels, this sort of man is morally disoriented and — for all his rhetorical skill — not a little trivial. It is the woman who absorbs the pain of difficult choices, and she does so with dignity. Her drama is a domestic one.

In a letter to his publisher Jurgenson (February, 1878), Tchaikovsky shared his own hopes for *Eugene Onegin*. He was eager that parts for the opera be made available as soon as possible, even before the première. 'This opera, it seems to me, will sooner have its success in *homes* and, if you will, on the concert stage than on the grand stage,' Tchaikovsky wrote. 'The success of this opera must begin from the bottom up, and not from the top down. That is, it is not the *theatre* that will make it known to the public, but, on the contrary, the public, little by little becoming familiar with it, will come to love it, and then the *theatre* will stage the opera in order to satisfy a demand of the public.'

There could not be a more accurate expression of the private space, domestic values, and fragmentable performance that Tchaikovsky envisioned for his 'lyrical scenes'. And in this way the composer, while fully resisting Pushkin's irony, displays a curious fidelity to Pushkin's text. The original *Eugene Onegin* — which Pushkin called a 'free novel' — had emerged in instalments over a number of years. Its readers, experiencing these successive fragments, matured along with the novel's protagonists. The intimate, open-ended scenes that Tchaikovsky desired for his listening public had been part of Pushkin's agenda for his *Onegin* as well.

The peasants in Andrei Serban's 1978 production for Welsh National Opera, designed by Michael Yeargan. photo: Julian Sheppard

Tchaikovsky's 'Eugene Onegin'

Roland John Wiley

Hope always draws the soul from the beauty which is seen to what is beyond, always kindles the desire for the hidden through what is constantly perceived.

— Gregory of Nyssa

'Onegin' as drama

Russians have always esteemed *Eugene Onegin*. Is it, in Boris Asafiev's hyperbole from *Symphonic Etudes*, a flower of the field, 'one of those rare works of art which so integrally enters into life and intertwines with life so closely that the two together become a vital, inevitable fact . . . which affectionately warms the spirit'? Let us consider the relationship of drama to music in an attempt to answer these questions.

Like Mussorgsky in *Boris Godunov*, Tchaikovsky and his co-librettist Konstantin Shilovsky retained in *Onegin* large segments of Pushkin's text, adapted Pushkin's words in other passages, and relocated many lines in their libretto. This produced a story with distinctive theatrical attributes, which are discussed in the other essays in this Guide. In the process of adaptation, Tchaikovsky made the subject his own. The composer's direct emotional engagement with the characters and the demands of the theatre take precedence over the poet's more detached view. For example, in Tchaikovsky, Lensky's behaviour at Tatyana's name-day party is much less discreet than in Pushkin. Lensky creates a public scene, whereas in the poem he leaves the party when Olga refuses him the cotillion in favour of Onegin, resolves to challenge his friend, delivers his note the next day, sees Olga again after that, and duels only the second morning after the party. In the opera Tatyana is tempted for a moment to act on her love for Onegin when he declares himself at the end. In Pushkin she never wavers in her fidelity to her husband. Tchaikovsky also specified the characters' ages more closely than Pushkin had: Onegin is 22, Lensky 19, Tatyana 17, Madame Larina 56, the nurse 70, and Gremin 45. These details, preserved in the composer's draft of the libretto, were not published in the score.

Character study is central to both poem and opera. The change of medium, however, prevented Tchaikovsky from following all the beautiful digressions on character which Pushkin scattered throughout the poem. Instead, the composer focusses on Tatyana, Lensky, and Onegin in Acts One, Two and Three respectively. Of these Tchaikovsky loved Tatyana most. She was, in the composer's description to Nadezhda von Meck:

> . . . . full of the pure feminine beauty of a maidenly soul, still not touched by contact with real life; hers is a dreamlike nature, vaguely seeking an ideal and passionately driving after it. Seeing nothing approaching her ideal, she remains calm but unsatisfied. But it had only to happen that a person appear who in externals stands apart from the milieu of the common-provincial, and she imagined this tò be her ideal, and she is overcome with passion.

'In real life', Madame Larina explains to Tatyana, 'I came to see that there

17

Anna Pollak as Madame Larina and Olwen Price as Filippyevna in the 1952 Sadler's Wells production by George Devine, designed by Motley (photo: Angus McBean © Harvard Theatre Collection)

are no heroes.' And there is none in the opera. But contact with 'real life' in the form of actions by Onegin destroys Tatyana's dreams in the first act and Lensky's in the second; in the third, Tatyana's commitment to 'real life' shatters Onegin. This process is set in motion because the lovers seem to be mismatched: Lensky loves Olga, Tatyana loves Onegin. 'Surely you aren't in love with the younger one?' Onegin queries Lensky in the quartet, 'I would have chosen the other one if I had been, like you, a poet!' Onegin is right, and such plot as develops in the opera bears out his remark. *Onegin* is a tale of what might have been had events been ever so slightly different or fate the least bit kinder. 'Happiness was so close', sing Tatyana and Onegin in the final duet.

For the empiricist the attribution of any occurrence to fate is unacceptable. Human events are determined by human actions. For Tchaikovsky, if his letters accurately reflect his beliefs, fate was a controlling factor in human affairs which might seem to be attributable to pure chance, and over which a person's actions had little influence. In *Onegin*, fate thus functions in two ways. It is called upon to explain events unpersuasively explained by chance. How is it, for instance, that Onegin happens to visit Madame Larina's estate in the first place? Fate also interacts with society's rules and customs. A character vexed by the tension between the expectations of social ritual and the temptation to thwart them will rationalize a course of action by invoking fate. Much of Tatyana's distress in the letter scene can be traced to this tension, placed in relief by her conversations with the nurse, who has never challenged expectations. But Tatyana does not escape fate by yielding to social pressure. When she rejects Onegin in the last act she is acting out of moral duty, a duty which fate has placed upon her by her marriage and which comes before desires of the heart. Nowhere in *Onegin* does the pressure to conform seem greater than in the duel scene. Neither man despises the other or wants to kill him; both acknowledge that their enmity is superficial and ask themselves if they should not burst out laughing and part friends before blood is spilled. They don't, and social ritual becomes the agency of fate.

Appreciating *Onegin* rests with understanding the rich complexities as expressed by the aspirations of the characters. Tchaikovsky (like Pushkin) illuminates the universal traits of the characters, and through them ponders the nature of beauty and creativity. Some parts of the opera are straightforward; others, 'untheatrical' and 'lacking in action' (Tchaikovsky's terms), challenge us to seek beyond what is immediately perceived.

Act One
In the orchestral introduction Tatyana's theme [1a] is presented first in single phrases, then in sequence. The stronger, richer variant of this theme [1b], which occurs repeatedly later in the Act, hints at the strength of character beneath Tatyana's demure exterior.

The first scene has a simple structure in three parts: the opening tableau in Madame Larina's garden, the interlude with the peasants, and the visit of Lensky and Onegin. This visit, preceded by Olga's short aria about herself, serves as an exposition of the characters. The visit also advances the narrative from absolute dramatic stasis to a point where it is possible for Tatyana to write her letter.

The opening tableau is remarkable for the lack of excitement when the curtain goes up. There is no crowd, no movement, no engaging stage business to arrest the eye or ear. Two activities are proceeding at once, neither of which

Thomas Allen as Onegin and Mirella Freni as Tatyana at the San Francisco Opera in 1986 (photo: David Powers)

seems very important: Madame Larina and the nurse are making jam, and the two girls are singing inside the house [2]. Activity without underlying dramatic momentum establishes the calm of our starting point, utter eventlessness awaiting an event.

On closer examination, we discover that something *is* happening, a counterpoint of music and dramatic motif. Tatyana's and Olga's duet, added by the librettists, is composed to Pushkin's poem 'The Singer'. A voice is heard in the quiet of the night, a singer of love and sorrow: have you heard the voice? Did you affirm his feelings with a quiet sigh of resignation? The reference to creativity, to the singer, to the 'sound of his fife, simple and melancholy'*, pointed by Pushkin's use of *svirel'*, the Russian for 'panpipes' in descriptions of pastoral scenes of ancient Greece, brings hints of Hellenic classicism to the first words we hear in the opera. Could this be an invocation of the muse, in which Tchaikovsky is referring to himself as the 'singer' of the opera, or possibly an allusion to the poet Lensky and his melancholy fate? The connection between this duet and Tatyana is indisputable: at the high point of each verse Tchaikovsky states the theme of the introduction, soon to be identified explicitly with her.

Simultaneously Madame Larina and the nurse sing their duet. From the casual recollections of two mature women about their younger days we learn that Madame Larina was married to Larin despite her preference for another man, and that household duties compensated for love throughout her marriage. 'God sends us habit from above in place of happiness and love,' they sing. The motif of loveless marriage sustained by a sense of duty will return in

---

* In David Lloyd-Jones's translation, this reference is lost but the Arcadian atmosphere of the song is still clear: 'within the grove each day the shepherd sings his plaintive song of love.'

Anja Silja as Tatyana, Elisabeth Steiner as Olga, David Rendall as Lensky and Bernd Weikl as Onegin in the Hamburg State Opera production by Adolf Dresen, designed by Karl-Ernst Hermann and Margit Bárdy, 1979 (photo: Gert von Bassewitz)

this Act when Tatyana talks to the nurse, and again in Act Three to determine the outcome of the opera. For the moment it serves as a foil for the girls' song, the unnoticed chatter of reality sounding in counterpoint to the voice of artistic reverie.

Peasants come to celebrate the harvest. Their first song [3] is a *protyazhnaya pesnya* or 'extended song', in which the chorus responds to the opening phrase sung by a soloist; it is about unrequited love. The second is a *khorovod* [4] about a pretty girl and a handsome lad. These choruses forecast the different characters of Tatyana and Olga, a contrast supported by Olga's own aria [5]. Behind the second chorus is a subtler message, which links it as well as the first with Tatyana. The man coming across the bridge carries a cudgel, and the threat is heightened because one of the girls must come out of the house to see him.* Is this a presentiment of Onegin's arrival? It may be an intentional substitute for the prophecy the poet offers Tatyana in Pushkin ('Dear Tanya, you're condemned to perish; / but first, the dreams that hope can cherish / evoke for you a sombre bliss . . .'), which the librettists omitted. 'How I love to hear the people singing, for music makes me lose myself in endless yearning for something far away,' is Tatyana's guileless response.

Lensky and Onegin arrive. After Onegin is introduced, the principals sing a quartet full of intimate revelations. For a moment dramatic time pauses as if to absorb the shock of this unexpected event. The two men carry on a dialogue in which Onegin chides his friend for choosing the wrong girl; Tatyana admits that she is smitten with Onegin; while Olga remains, as she will throughout the opera, largely unaware of the deeper motivations of the other characters:

* See page 59.

she points out that Onegin's visit will set the neighbours gossiping. This ensemble mirrors the opening scene in the joining of two duets to form a quartet, and in the understated presentation of important ideas. Tatyana's admission prepares us for the letter scene, and the fatal conflict between Lensky and Onegin over Olga is adumbrated as Lensky almost takes offence at his friend's derogatory remarks.

After the quartet Lensky pairs off with Olga, Onegin with Tatyana. Consumed by the ardour of a poet, Lensky first formally, then intimately (by changing the form of the second person) proclaims his love for Olga [6]. She is sympathetic but not swept up in Lensky's transport except to respond, with more portent than she realizes, to his use of the word 'vechnost' (*lit.* eternity) to describe the 24 hours since he last saw her. Called upon in the score to sing 'with cool politeness', Onegin nevertheless opens with a lyrical phrase [7], and tells Tatyana that he too was once a dreamer. By having him sing this melody again a few moments later when referring to his dead uncle, Tchaikovsky makes it an expression of his well-polished behaviour in polite company. This use of the music downgrades the warm initial connotations of the theme to an empty formula of social discourse.

In Pushkin, Tatyana falls in love with Onegin after a period of longing to fall in love, and waits an unspecified time before writing to him. In the opera her mood is established when she tells of the highly emotional effect of the book she is reading; she responds to Onegin as in Pushkin, but writes to him (according to Tchaikovsky's draft libretto) a few days later. Her conversations with her nurse, which enclose the letter scene, point up her emotional turmoil — by turns painful and exalted.

Gabriela Beňačková as Tatyana and Patricia Payne as Filippyevna at Covent Garden, 1979 (photo: Donald Southern)

Tchaikovsky organizes the music of Scene Two (like many other sections of the opera) according to strophic principles similar to those of Wagner's music dramas. The strophes are not identical, but have enough in common (theme, keys, or sequence of ideas) to provide a strong sense of symmetry with one another. Typically he will mark the beginning of each strophe with a distinctive melody, and continue with new music appropriate to the flow of meaning in the text.

He builds the first exchange between Tatyana and the nurse as follows:

Introduction. 'Tatyana alone' [8] 'Tatyana' [1b]; the nurse arrives to see Tatyana to bed.
Strophe 1. The nurse's response to Tatyana's 'So tell me more about the past'; nurse's theme [9] in the orchestra, with 'Tatyana' as subsidiary theme.
Strophe 2. The nurse's response to Tatyana's 'Then why did you get married?'; nurse's theme in her vocal part.
Bridge to Letter Scene. 'Tatyana's anguish' [10].
Strophe 1. Tatyana: 'Oh nanny, I'm so wretched!', [10] in Tatyana's part.
Strophe 2. Tatyana: 'I am not ill . . . I'm in love', [10] in orchestra, [9] as subsidiary theme.

The Letter Scene is constructed along similar lines:

Introduction [10] with new theme [11].
First pair of strophes [12]: Tatyana begins to write and then breaks off.
Second pair of strophes [13]: Tatyana pledges herself to Onegin.
A new theme in this section [14] forms a bridge to the new musical peroration which closes the scene.

For all its passion, Tatyana's letter acknowledges fate, 'the will of heaven', and her vow to submit to it. 'Vsya zhizn' moya byla zalogom, / Svidan'ya vernovo s toboi' (lit. 'All my life has been a pledge of this inevitable meeting with you,') she writes. But if Tatyana is submissive, she isn't blind. She realises that Onegin is in large part a vision conjured up by her own musings, and with commanding perspective on her own emotions of the moment, she refers to him at the beginning of the scene as a 'fatal tempter', and at the end asks: (lit.) 'Who are you? My guardian angel or an insidious tempter?', a line which Tchaikovsky offsets with a new melody [14]. That she intuitively understands the emotional risk she is taking prepares us for the end of this Act and the end of the opera. Prediction is one dramatic function of the Letter Scene.

Another is to reveal Tatyana's exceptional personality. If she is impressionable and impulsive, Tatyana is not immature. The conviction of her feelings and her constancy will prove lasting, and she already has the experience of tempering passion with patience and suffering.

She goes to her window, draws the curtain, and the morning light streams in with a swelling crescendo in the orchestra. The oboe and bassoon play bucolic solos [15] as Tatyana sings, 'There goes the shepherd . . . / The world's at peace.' Are these not the panpipes, are these not the shepherd and the brightness of a morning in that Arcadian landscape suggested in the sisters' opening duet? Suddenly Tatyana finds herself miscast in paradise, a melancholy singer in a carefree world. By distinguishing Tatyana's thoughts from the reality of her physical surroundings, Tchaikovsky prepares us for her

Evelyn Lear as Tatyana, San Francisco, 1971 (photo: Ken Howard)

encounter with Onegin; by creating a link with the beginning of the work, he again makes us aware of the delicate symmetries which unify his apparently disparate 'lyrical scenes'. The sunrise at the end of the letter scene, and Tatyana's words 'I long for you!' ('Ya zhdu tebya', *lit.* 'I await you'), also anticipate the duel scene.

The nurse returns. When Tatyana calls upon her to send a message to Onegin (a dialogue based on [16]), she never quite grasps the situation. As Scene Two closes do we hear the echo of Shakespeare in the sunrise, a befuddled nurse who talks of marriage and sees to messages, and a young girl in whom impulse and wisdom are combined?

The girls' chorus [17] which opens Scene Three recalls the first chorus of Scene One. There the song was of the harvest, here of picking berries. But the dramatic function is different: this chorus sustains the lighthearted Arcadian atmosphere established by the woodwind [15] at the end of the letter scene. It represents the apparent utopia that surrounds Tatyana as she deals with her own realities.

Onegin's response to Tatyana's letter is an avowal which is not only troubling to her but, in Tchaikovsky's presentation of it, potentially troubling to us. The words of his explanation are not disdainful but almost affectionate: were he destined for marriage, Tatyana would be his bride. Yet he is not: 'But I'm not made for warm affection, / And as for wedlock, even less,' and he imagines a marriage not unlike the one Madame Larina described in the opening tableau. Onegin's music, however, has the same ambivalence in its expressiveness that it had in Scene One. Again he is called upon to sing 'somewhat coldly', again Tchaikovsky gives him a lyrical melody [18 and 19], and again the listener comes away wondering if the sentiments expressed were heartfelt or merely dutiful and engagingly polite. Will he ever be moved in the way Tatyana was? Her wordless reaction to his speech compounds the ambiguities of the scene. What might she have said? Her silence, and the close of Act One, understated and without a strong sense of finality, forestall answers to those questions.

Act Two

The orchestral introduction is devoted to a single theme [14] from the letter scene, which accompanied Tatyana's question, 'Are you an angel sent to guard me / Or will you tempt and then discard me?' In this scene Onegin will appear to Lensky to be Olga's 'tempter'.

The action of Scene One is unambiguous. Onegin is irritated by the women's gossip about him, and decides to take vengeance on Lensky (who brought him to the party) by flirting with Olga. Lensky is incensed, a quarrel ensues, Lensky challenges Onegin to a duel.

The curtain rises on a choral waltz [20] which draws on the tradition of dances in French opera and is indebted in particular to the waltz in Gounod's *Faust*. Unlike the purely spectacular divertissements of Russian classics like Glinka's *A Life for the Tsar* (1836) and Borodin's *Prince Igor* (1890), these dances merge drama with spectacle. Friction between Onegin and Lensky develops over Olga dancing so much with Onegin. Lensky expresses his pique, but the waltz ends, leaving him without any distracting activity to cover his words. He next turns to Olga, confronts her with her coquetry and claims that she no longer loves him. But Onegin interrupts this exchange to accompany Olga in the cotillion, and Lensky is frustrated again.

Another distraction is the appearance of Monsieur Triquet, who sings

Francis Egerton as Monsieur Triquet and Lilian Sukis as Tatyana in David Pountney's production for Scottish Opera, designed by Roger Butlin and Deirdre Clancy, 1979 (photo: Eric Thorburn)

couplets dedicated to Tatyana on this, her nameday. In Pushkin Triquet is a 'modish gentleman, recently from Tambov' (a contradiction, since 'modish gentlemen' do not come from the Urals), outlandishly attired in a red peruke, who has refashioned children's verses into Tatyana's couplets. Tchaikovsky has taken from Pushkin the Frenchman's exterior aspect, but he elaborates and changes the significance of the character. Of the two sets of couplets the composer wrote for Triquet (as published in the Collected Works Edition of Tchaikovsky's music), the first is macaronic in French and broken, almost illiterate (but funny), Russian; it is a bit of comic scene painting, as in Pushkin, in which Tchaikovsky mimics someone struggling with the Russian language. The second, all in French, is fluent and lovely*. Triquet invites the guests to contemplate Tatyana's charm and beauty, and likens her to a star which illuminates both days and nights. 'Brillez, brillez toujours, belle Tatyaná!' he sings, keeping a touch of affectation in the final accent.

The transformation of Triquet's scene from a 14-line episode in Pushkin (without couplets) into a song of aria-like pretensions invites explanation. The style of his music — the *galant* phrases which accompany his entrance and the unabashedly Mediterranean consonance of the borrowed tune 'Dormez, dormez, chères amours' [21] — might suggest that this interlude is another static, ornamental scene like the one with which the opera began. Except to

---

* Tchaikovsky did not specify which set of couplets (possibly both) should be performed. The first set is surely intended for Russian audiences; the second is suitable for any operatic audience and is the only set that Triquet sings in most productions outside Russia.

Claes-Haaken Ahnsjö as Lensky at Tatyana's name-day party in the 1977 production by Rudolf Noelte, designed by Jürgen Rose at the Bayerische Staatsoper, Munich (photo: Sabine Toepffer)

prolong Lensky's frustration, it seems to stand apart from the main business of the drama.

By troubling to write *two* sets of couplets, however, Tchaikovsky hinted at another purpose. The relationship between the disjointed, ungrammatical words of the first set and the elegant language of the second affects our view of Triquet, transformed from a ridiculous dandy into a fair poet. For the first time in *Onegin*, a singer of songs is presented to us directly on stage, and he sings of Tatyana as an inspiration for poetry. In effect, he is declaring her to be a muse.

The cotillion [22] is put off until Triquet is finished, and Lensky's anger festers during the delay. Onegin dances his turn with Olga, then takes her to her seat. He spots Lensky, and the quarrel recommences as Onegin chides his friend for sulking. At first Lensky maintains control, but as his reproaches grow more indiscreet the other guests notice and stop dancing. In a moment they have surrounded the two men. As he loses control, Lensky in succession declares Onegin not to be his friend, insults him, demands satisfaction, and challenges him to a duel.

Madame Larina pleads against violence in her house. Repeating the words 'Here in your house' (sung to a variant of [6], his love song in Act One), Lensky initiates the long finale [23], during which Onegin expresses remorse, Tatyana jealousy and anguish, and Olga just joins some of the guests who remark on the men's behaviour and fear that a duel might in fact ensue. Onegin declares Lensky to be out of his mind, but stands ready to accept his challenge. Lensky bids farewell to Olga 'forever' (a touching echo of the word 'endless' in his

Benjamin Luxon as Onegin and Nicolai Gedda as Lensky at Covent Garden in 1982 (photo: Christina Burton)

address to her in Act One), and the scene ends in an uproar.

From his farewell to Olga and throughout Scene Two, it is clear that Lensky is not out of his mind, but responding to the dictates of fate. Tchaikovsky tells us as much in Lensky's words in this scene (his anger is completely dissipated, replaced by utter resignation) and in the music, starting with the orchestral introduction [23]. Such a clear reference to the beginning of *Rigoletto*, where the doom of the principal character is represented by similar fanfares, hardly seems accidental.

It is dawn in wintertime. Lensky laments his lost youth [25]. Onegin arrives; the adversaries sing a duet [26] as their seconds complete formalities. Lensky and Onegin avoid each other's eyes but their sentiments, presented musically in near-perfect canon, are exactly the same. They are less angry than incredulous that unreasoning fate has made them enemies, and helpless to stop what is about to happen. Again we hear the beginning of Lensky's love song to Olga [6], transformed, as the pistols are handed out. A moment later Lensky is dead.

His death seems to be the tragic event foreshadowed in the opera's opening duet. As Scene Two ends other connections between Tatyana and Lensky come to mind, parallels between the letter scene and the duel. Lensky's soliloquy, like Tatyana's, is an apostrophe to a loved one. Both scenes end at sunrise, and are marked by the exclamation, 'Ya zhdu tebya!' ('I await you!') Perhaps most strikingly, Tchaikovsky emphasizes the affinity of Lensky and Tatyana by making the principal melody of Lensky's aria [25] an unmistakable variant of the important melody in the letter scene [14] to which Tatyana wondered if Onegin were angel or seducer — Onegin, who in his offhand remark first linked them and who has brought misery to them both. Act Two is framed by the unstated influence of Onegin, because this melody of Tatyana's is the first music heard in it, and Lensky's melody the last.

The tragedy of Lensky's death may be argued as more central to the philosophical message of the opera than that of Tatyana's unhappiness. Pushkin and Tchaikovsky both see the spark of creativity in Lensky, and value above all his vivid appreciation of the beautiful, and his purity of heart.

Dénes Gulyás as Lensky and Thomas Allen as Onegin, San Francisco, 1986 (photo: Marty Sohl)

The Act Three polonaise in David Pountney's production for Scottish Opera, designed by Roger Butlin and Deirdre Clancy, 1979 (photo: Eric Thorburn)

Act Three

While continuing and completing the narrative, Tchaikovsky in Act Three also draws parallels with what has come before. The sizeable gap in time and circumstance which separates it from the first two Acts allows him to make it a summary as well as a fulfilment. But it is a summary full of ironic reversal, at the heart of which lies the central irony of the drama: Onegin, who has caused the suffering of others, will presently be his own victim.

The irony becomes apparent as soon as the curtain rises. A dance is in progress [27], as it was at the beginning of Act Two, part of a ball at which Tatyana is again a prominent attraction and Onegin a casual guest. But much has changed: Onegin is now the frustrated lover, Tatyana the object of his affection, and Prince Gremin the self-assured older man.

Onegin has, arguably, changed the most. Still bored, he is experiencing genuine remorse for the first time in the opera — anguish about his life, its wasted past and present lack of purpose. Then Tatyana enters [28], radiant if subdued, now Princess Gremina. As Tatyana was instantly smitten with Onegin in Act One, so in Act Three the reverse is true. While neither poet nor composer makes explicit reference to the possibility, Onegin's self-reproach may have made him especially vulnerable to inspiration at the sight of Tatyana. She is now *his* muse, and that adds to the ironic effect.

Prince Gremin is Onegin's old friend who, before presenting friend to wife, sings an aria about her [29]. He describes the salutary effects of love (ironic in the wake of Onegin's rediscovery) and then, in a distinct recollection of Triquet's apostrophe, describes Tatyana as a ray of sunlight, a bright star on a clear night, an angel.

Gremin introduces him; Tatyana, her old feelings revived, claims to be tired and asks to leave. Onegin now reproaches himself for his behaviour toward her before, then expresses his passion. She alone can give meaning to his life. At this point Tchaikovsky gives him a prominent theme from the Letter Scene [11], set to a paraphrase of the text Tatyana sang. The immediate effect is to show the unity of feeling between the characters, but here too there is an ironic twist: that Onegin, more jaded than ever, should still be so far behind Tatyana in reaching the point where *her* feelings were when she wrote her letter years before.

The second scene of Act Three is a reckoning, as the last scenes of each Act have been. Another letter has been sent, with much the same purpose as the first, but Onegin is the author. Tatyana is distressed and crying as she reads it [30], and with the words 'As long ago now, young and tender-hearted' we hear her theme [1a] for the first time since Act One.

Onegin enters. Tatyana breaks the silence she was unable to break when he addressed her at the end of Act One. She does not so much reproach him for rejecting her before as question the honour of his motives in asking her to be unfaithful now. This is the worst irony of all: Onegin's passion, however genuine, cannot reclaim his reputation for incapacity to feel. His sincerity now, like Tatyana's before, counts for nothing.

A moment for decisive action has come, and once again the principals invoke fate. Tatyana confesses that she still loves Onegin, but the opportunity for happiness together has passed. She believes that he is a man of honour [31], but neither the past nor the present can be changed. She stands firm, and Onegin runs out in despair.

Tchaikovsky was uncertain for a time about how best to end the opera. In his first version Tatyana struggled with the temptation to join Onegin, and in her anguish claimed to be dying. Gremin appeared and with a gesture ordered Onegin away, to which he responded, 'O death, I go to seek thee out!' and ran

Helen Field as Tatyana, David Gwynne as Prince Gremin and Phillip Joll as Onegin in the production by Andrei Serban, designed by Michael Yeargan, for Welsh National Opera in 1978.

Eugenia Moldoveanu as Tatyana with Yuri Masurok as Onegin, Covent Garden, 1980 (photo: Donald Southern)

off. A piano-vocal score of this version was published, but without any words set beneath Onegin's closing melody. Only with the second edition does Onegin sing his final line as we now know it.

The ending of Onegin is abrupt and open-ended; it could not be otherwise. With Tatyana's decision to remain faithful to Gremin, the drama has been played out: we know what she feels about Onegin, and she has given herself up to a life of habit, not of romantic love. Lensky is dead and Olga is married to another man (although Tchaikovsky omits any reference to this). And Onegin, who has shown us no sense of purpose up to now, must continue indefinitely living with this flaw. There is no peroration because there is so little sense of catharsis, so little on which to build a summation. It simply ends.

Hidden and perceived in Tchaikovsky's music
'Operatic symphonism' is the term by which some authorities have attempted to account for the relationship of music to words and drama in *Onegin*. It means, in the broadest sense, that Tchaikovsky's music is continuously responsive to narrative and character portrayal while avoiding routine operatic formulas of any kind. We have already observed how themes provide direct and indirect coherence. Tatyana's melody [1a and 1b] is used

unambiguously as a leitmotif in Act One, whereas the thematic relationship which likens her to Lensky [14 and 25] is expressed in subtle melodic variants. Such devices promote unity — an unquestionable virtue — but the more central difficulty in *Onegin* is providing variety, a problem which originates in the lack of polar contrasts and ongoing tensions in the story. One solution involves a readily perceived distinction between types of music. Another, involving key, is hidden. Together they make *Onegin* symphonic.

The three types of music (as formulated by the late Soviet musicologist Nadezhda Tumanina) are lyrical, scene-setting, and fateful. Lyricism is pre-eminent in the music of the three principal characters, who at any given moment are moving from neutral or tentative recitative-like themes to fully contoured aria-like melodies. Tatyana's lyrical music expresses her strength and genuineness of feeling, and gives credibility to the letter scene. In Lensky, who seems always on the verge of extremes of feeling, the lyrical is native to his poetical sensitivities. Onegin's lyricism is more guarded, and only emerges in full flower when his feelings do likewise in Act Three.

Lyricism is the foremost means of expressing heightened emotions in *Onegin*, but it may be affected by the reluctance of characters to let their feelings be known. In such cases the orchestra may provide lyrical music while a character's emotions (and vocal lines) become liberated. This occurs in the letter scene, for example, where the orchestra introduces important themes [12, 14] as if presenting thoughts that come into Tatyana's mind before she gives them verbal expression.

Scene-setting music is what the term implies, with connotations of ethnic character. Tchaikovsky uses it to distinguish the countryside from St Petersburg in music: in Act One by the peasant choruses, in Act Two by the choral waltz and the mazurka, and in Act Three by the polonaise and écossaise. Fateful music is brief and strategically placed; it consists of loud, dissonant, mostly harsh sonorities which anticipate fate's work at the beginning of Act One, Scene Two (leading to the Letter Scene), Act Two, Scene Two (the duel), and Act Three, Scene Two (as the curtain rises on Tatyana with Onegin's letter).

Interwoven among these devices in *Onegin* is a complex and ingenious system of keys with which Tchaikovsky reinforces its narrative and philosophical message. To be sure, this aspect of *Onegin* is subtle. The composer never referred to it, and while we may sense the key relationships immediately, our appreciation of their contribution to unity in the opera increases with reflection and study. In effect, the relationships which exist between keys and modes in the opera as keys and modes can form, through association, analogies with situations and characters. The system of keys in *Onegin* centres around two sets of associations. One applies to the basic premises of the opera:

G minor: the country (the opening scene)
E minor: fate (the key of Lensky's aria, and of the end of the opera as Tatyana refuses Onegin)
C# minor: Lensky's death (the pointless squandering of beauty)

Another series of relationships, similar to the first except based on major keys, is established within Act One:

G major: arrival of Onegin
E major: Lensky's love for Olga
Db major: Tatyana; the Letter Scene

The first and third keys within each group are based on opposite scales. No two keys in regular use can be any further removed from one another than these. When we extend this relationship of music theory to the opera, key reinforces situation: Lensky's death is a break with the harmony of the country scene (in Pushkin's and Tchaikovsky's view, it also affects the wellspring of creative life); and Onegin's arrival is ominous for Tatyana.

The middle keys of each grouping are equidistant from the outer ones, and their associations are appropriate to this relationship: fate interrupts country life to bring about Lensky's death, but in the beginning Lensky is the intermediary whereby Tatyana first meets Onegin. (The association of fate with E minor may be observed elsewhere in Tchaikovsky's music, such as *Francesca di Rimini*, the Fifth Symphony, and *The Sleeping Beauty*.)

In addition, certain relationships between the groupings are also illuminating because some keys in one group share the same scale with a key in the other but are based on a different tonal centre. E major and C# minor are two such relative keys, and suggest the proximity, appearances notwithstanding, of Lensky's death to his love for Olga. G major and E minor also share the same scale, and make the critical connection between fate and Onegin's initial visit to Madame Larina's estate. Elsewhere in the opera Tchaikovsky uses relative keys to bring about a sense of ironic reversal. Onegin's response to Tatyana in Scene Three, for example, is in B♭ major, the relative of G minor and country life. And when Onegin and Tatyana in Act Three sing 'Happiness was once so near us!' Tchaikovsky moves to B♭ minor, the relative of D♭ major, Tatyana's key.

Keys separated by a semitone, also distantly related to one another, are yet another means by which Tchaikovsky reinforces dramatic nuance. In the Letter Scene, for example, the principal key of D♭ is juxtaposed with episodes in keys a semitone on either side, C major and D minor. All three are coordinated with Tatyana's changes of mood, C major for rapturous flights of fancy, D minor for moments of sober reality, and D♭ for the expression of her vulnerability. These associations continue throughout the opera: the A major of the girls' chorus at the beginning and the end of Scene Three may be taken as a dominant function of D minor, and represent reality in the context of Tatyana's musings (it echoes the A major of the nurse's stories of the past before the Letter Scene). After Lensky's death, Tchaikovsky returns to D minor to end the Act, not the E minor of Lensky's aria or the C# minor of the death itself, as if to bring us back, benumbed, to what is real — sunrise on a grey, muddy, frozen day. The key of Tatyana at the ball is D♭; she is still a vulnerable Tatyana, and she is tempted for a moment (also in D♭) to give in to Onegin's entreaties. How appropriate, in this context, is Tchaikovsky's shift to D major just for Tatyana's 'I love you', a touching moment of reality in this emotionally turbulent scene.

Tchaikovsky's use of E minor shows us how fate intervenes to shape the tragic outcomes of Acts Two and Three. At the party in Act Two, Onegin's decision to punish Lensky by flirting with Olga is wilful, and is pointed by his dancing the cotillion with her after Lensky had asked her for that dance. The cotillion thus begins in G major, Onegin's key. No sooner has an interlude in the dance given Onegin the opportunity to make fun of Lensky than Tchaikovsky moves to E minor, for this is the moment when Onegin yields control over events to fate. Lensky's burst of anger cannot be subdued by Onegin or anyone else, and leads to the challenge and the duel. In Act Three Tchaikovsky does not move decisively to the key of fate until Tatyana

Act One, Scene Two (above) and Scene Three (below) of the Kirov production, directed by Maxim Krastin and Yuri Temirkanov and designed by Igor Ivanov, which was performed at the Royal Opera House, Covent Garden in 1987 (photo: The Kirov Opera)

overcomes the temptation to go with Onegin and resolves to remain faithful to Gremin. Hers is a wilful act, but represents to Onegin the fateful outcome of a sequence of her actions over which he yielded control when he rejected her in Act One.

The principal virtue of Tchaikovsky's key system is to establish and emphasize the kinds of contrasts which are understated in the libretto. The keys also enrich the music in other ways, especially in Act Three. That Tchaikovsky moves directly and emphatically to Db major when Tatyana enters in that Act affirms that she is the same person she was at the end of the letter scene. When Onegin borrows Tatyana's text and melody from the letter scene, it is relevant that he sings in Bb major, for that was the key of his rebuff to Tatyana in Act One. The choice deepens the rich stream of irony which runs through the Act.

Tchaikovsky treats the final scene of the opera with special care. It opens with Tatyana in the key of Lensky's death singing a melody which mimics that of the aria her husband has just sung (compare [30] with [29]) while she sorrows over the letter she has just received from the man she really loves. Tragedy and responsibility and passion are all concentrated here. For a moment, when Tatyana sings that Onegin is honourable [31], the key of the Letter Scene returns. As we have just observed, however, when she resolves to remain true to her husband, Tchaikovsky moves to E minor.

Key is but one of the complex dimensions of *Onegin* which deserves closer scrutiny. Speech rhythms, folk intonations, and orchestration also contribute to the labyrinth of relationships which bind together these 'lyrical scenes after Pushkin'. But, in the end, *Onegin* is only partly remarkable for the finesse and power of its artistry. It survives by the eloquence with which Tchaikovsky illuminated the tragedy hidden behind a death in the country and a life misspent in St Petersburg.

Note: the citations from Pushkin in this article are given in Charles Johnston's translation.

An Appreciation of 'Eugene Onegin'

Natalia Challis

'. . . We are such stuff
As dreams are made of . . .'
— *The Tempest*

As Shakespeare illuminates the whole of English culture, its inner life and nuances and aspirations, so Pushkin and Tchaikovsky give us an insight into Russian life and its ideals. All three artists share a capacity for love and sense of humanity.

The creative essence of Pushkin's art was best expressed by Dostoevsky, who in his own work perhaps more than any other writer spoke of the conflict of Russian culture with western; but he also saw the two united in the grace of Pushkin's poetry, and in Pushkin's ability to understand and express the human condition regardless of nationality. This universality is present in Tchaikovsky's music when he re-conceives in western forms the Russian *pésennaya kul'túra*. This term for the types of expression in Russian song refers

P. Khokhlov (Onegin) and M. Eichenwald (Tatyana) in the production by A. Barzal and K. Valz, at the Bolshoi Theatre, Moscow, 1889, (photo: Bolshoi Theatre Archives)

more broadly to how everyday life in Russia, its joys — love and marriage — and sorrows, such as parting and death, had an ancient cultural and ritual expression in song. By making use of this tradition, the art of both poet and composer does not withdraw from reality, but rather moves towards it, and we come to understand that certain dreams are alike, whether in rural Russia or on an island 'full of noises, sounds and sweet airs'.

It is a tradition among Russians to take *Eugene Onegin*, both poem and opera, as a means to understand and share the spirit of what is Russian. Pushkin's poetry and Tchaikovsky's music reflect our yearnings; we are companions in their artistic quest. We may even come to a discovery anticipated by neither poet nor musician, and experience something in their work of which they may not have been aware. All art possesses an inner freedom, the potential for interpretation which it offers its beholders. Through Prospero Shakespeare grants this freedom to his art, and in the last chapter of *Onegin* Pushkin too speaks of this inner freedom, which he could see but through a glass darkly when he began his poem. Pushkin described his art as a gift of grace, which he received freely and freely gave up again to his audience:

> In my childhood she loved me
> And handed me the flute of seven pipes,
> Smiling, she listened to me,
> And gently touching the sound holes of the hollow reed
> With my weak fingers, I played already then,
> Both solemn hymns inspired by the gods
> And songs of peaceful Phrygian shepherds.
>
> From morn till evening in the groves' mute shade
> I heeded diligently the secret maiden's words;
> And rejoicing me with unexpected favour,
> Having brushed the curls back from her sweet brow,
> She herself took the panpipes from my hands,
> The reed was animated by divine breath
> And my heart filled with sacred enchantment.

Pushkin *The Muse*

When *Eugene Onegin* was suggested to Tchaikovsky as a possible text for an opera he first demurred, then re-read the poem 'with delight', as he wrote, 'and spent an absolutely sleepless night, the result of which was the scenario of a charming opera with Pushkin's text . . .' 'What a deep mine of poetry there is in *Eugene Onegin!*' he continued later, 'I do not deceive myself, I know that there will be few theatrical effects in the opera. But the poetic richness everywhere, the humanity, the simplicity of narrative, together with the inspired text will readily overcome these defects. I am writing my music with great pleasure and I know with certainty that the poetic quality of the narrative and the ineffable beauty of the text will come through.'

Tchaikovsky wrote his music in rare consonance with the verbal and musical rhythms and the aesthetic of Pushkin's text. The expressiveness and suppleness of language in the poem are translated into a subtle feeling of harmoniousness which permeates the opera. Pushkin perceived sounds musically, as a true poet. The words of the poem fill it with sounds of nature — of changing seasons, leaves rustling in the wind, the cries of birds, crickets chirping in the fields. In the following passage, for example, Pushkin invokes an autumnal image by what is described:

The mysterious canopy of forests
With a sad rustle bared itself,
A mist settled on the field.
A caravan of honking geese
Stretched out towards the south . . .

Onegin, Chapter Four, LX

In Russian, the gait of the metre and the subtle repetitions of consonants 's',
'sh', and 'zh' actually replicate the rustling sound of the falling leaves, while
in the last two lines of the passage, the shift to consonantal stress on 'g' and 'k',
combined with the upward gesture implicit in looking from earth to sky and a
rise in tessitura, capture in sound the new image of the cackling geese:

Lesóv tainstvennaya sén'
S pechál'nym shúmon obnazhálas',
Lozhílsya na polyá tumán,
Guséi kriklivykh karaván
Tyanúlsya k yúgu . . .

The effect is not unlike the 'Spring Song' in Act One of Wagner's *The Valkyrie*,
where similar shifts of consonantal values coincide with changes in poetic
image. Sounds and voices of the city and the countryside are heard in this way
throughout Pushkin's poem. We hear, in Dostoevsky's phrase, the 'passing
choir of this earth'.

Tchaikovsky does not reproduce the fullness of Pushkin's world, for he
gives us only seven scenes, in which, with an impressionist's brush, he depicts
the quiet mood of late summer soon to be disturbed, the air of sadness of early
autumn, death in the stillness of deep winter, and hints of spring and hope —
beyond the end of the stage narrative. Hope is alluded to in Pushkin's poem
'The Singer', which Tchaikovsky chose as the text of the girls' duet at the
beginning of the opera. The poem echoes and replies to Gray's 'Elegy written
in a Country Churchyard', which was translated into Russian by Pushkin's
teacher, the poet Zhukovsky, whose version was considered a wellspring of
inspiration for Russian poets in the early nineteenth century. 'The Singer'
may be the key to understanding Tchaikovsky's concept of *Onegin*, for the
hope which lies at the heart of Gray's 'Elegy' is the hope for forgiveness and
the resurrection. Although we do not know Tchaikovsky's reason for choosing
'The Singer', this brief poem unquestionably adds a dimension to his work for
us to interpret.

Tchaikovsky strove for all possible fidelity to his libretto, set in the 1820s
(now called the Pushkin epoch), a time of classical simplicity of mood and
dress. It is an epoch which, for Russians, does not date, as we can appreciate
from the grace and poise of the unhurried round of country life, as much as
from the preserved architectural elegance of 'Pushkin's St Petersburg'.

Elements of *Onegin*, the poem and the opera, and events of Pushkin's life
become intertwined on stage. We are visually reminded of Pushkin's literary
presence in the first act, for the stage setting of the Larin home, the fields and
church beyond (as indicated in the libretto), depict Trigorskoye, an estate
owned by Pushkin's friends, not far from Pushkin's own home Mikhail-
ovskoye, by tradition taken to be the location of Onegin's 'charming village
manor'. The third act, in music and dance movement of simplicity and
grandeur, evokes the 'austere, harmonious aspect' of St Petersburg, beloved
by poet and composer (though at times they may have assured us otherwise).
And we also recall in the duel scene that Pushkin, like the young poet Lensky,

was to be mortally wounded in a duel in the snows of January. Throughout this scene, Tchaikovsky 'sings out' (as we speak of the Orthodox funeral service) the dreams of both poets, and this music may bring to mind Shakespeare's elegy for Hamlet:

> Good-night, sweet prince,
> And flights of angels sing thee to thy rest.

The opera thus presents to contemporary Russian viewers images from a very familiar tradition. At the time Tchaikovsky wrote the opera, Pushkin's poetry was considered a classic but did not enjoy the pre-eminence it does today. Poetry had been overshadowed by the prose of the Golden Age, the novels and inspired literary and art criticism, which reflects the often tempestuous aspirations of the middle of the century. Pushkin was considered a worthy poet who founded the literary language but who had been superseded by writers who were thought to have a fuller understanding of Russian needs and ideals. Only Turgenev, Dostoevsky and the poet-critic Apollon Grigoriev saw in him the qualities which, in time, became appreciated by a larger audience. Tchaikovsky in his opera of 1877-79 and Dostoevsky in his Pushkin Address of 1880 almost simultaneously brought to public attention the aesthetic and philosophic depth of *Eugene Onegin* — the composer in his reconception of the beauty and personal drama of the poem, the writer in his claim that it was an image of Russia's spiritual state.

Both the poem and the opera have a quality in common: simplicity. The Metropolitan Anastasy, a hierarch of the Russian church, wrote of Pushkin's gift:

> Pushkin approaches everything simply and naturally . . . He takes all reality as God gave it to us. Like a true artist he contemplates and depicts its scenes calmly and objectively. From this approach springs a childlike spontaneity, clarity, and the purity of his contemplation, the pastel-like lightness and transparency of his design, which make his work equally comprehensible to persons of all ages. We accept his images as simply and spontaneously as we do nature itself. This is that simplicity of genius or the genius of being simple. Together with artistic truth Pushkin everywhere seeks the truth as expressed by humankind, for one is inseparable from the other. He strives to be sincere both with himself and with his reader, which, as Carlyle expressed it, is the stamp of genius.

This is precisely what Tchaikovsky translated so well into music. By emulating not every detail of narrative, but rather Pushkin's simplicity of design and expression, Tchaikovsky preserved the essence of Pushkin's art.

* * *

'It is almost impossible to grasp the depth of meaning of Pushkin's words', wrote Anna Akhmatova, perhaps the greatest Russian poet of the twentieth century and a Pushkin scholar. Pushkin worked towards the creation of a 'metaphysical language', as he called it, which reveals man's spiritual life. Tchaikovsky responded with a richness of musical nuance fully equal to Pushkin's sensitivity to the philosophical associations of the poem. Through music he keeps faith with the poet's dramatic narrative.

Tchaikovsky gives the audience a sense of time as it is perceived by each

Anne Howells as Olga and Neil Rosenshein as Lensky, Covent Garden, 1986 (photo: Clive Barda)

individual in the opera. Onegin and Tatyana, Lensky and Olga, and all whose lives they touch, allude to their dreams and to their awareness of the passage of time in the realization of their dreams. Tchaikovsky emphasizes the words *mechtá*, a dream or ideal, and *mechtánie*, the process of dreaming, of desiring, and shows us how the protagonists reach their ideals, and how Onegin is unable to rise above the process of desire or dreaming. The choices they have made or must make comprise the opera's underlying dramatic tension, and some of the choices are to be resolved outside the narrative we see on stage.

Madame Larina and the nurse sing of the dreams of their youth, unfulfilled then, but now found in their home and family. Olga, in Pushkin's description, is 'always bright as the morn' and in the libretto confesses that she herself is 'like a carefree dream, full of the joy of life'. Lensky takes her for his Muse; she may be likened to the image of the cloudless classical poetry which inspired Pushkin in his youth. Lensky, who personifies the Romantic spirit, as encapsulated by Pushkin in his early poetry, loves the physical radiance of his Hellenistic muse. He is introspective, a man with deep emotions and passionate dreams. He compares himself to Onegin:

A wave and a stone,
Poetry and prose,
Ice and flame
Are not as different from each other
As are we.

41

Left: S. Lemechev as Lensky at the Bolshoi in 1933; right: Yuri Masurin as Lensky with the Kirov Opera in 1987 (photos: The Kirov Opera)

Pushkin places the passionate element of creativity in Lensky beside the cold worldliness of Onegin, which will devastate Lensky's dreams. The theme of inspiration destroyed by the worldly and the narrowly rational is also explored by Pushkin in his play *Mozart and Salieri*.

In Lensky's aria before the sunrise, in Act Two, Scene Two, Tchaikovsky presents the metaphysical language of Pushkin and the poet's suggestion that Lensky does achieve his ideal before dying with the realization that all is blessed in life and death:

> All is blessed: of vigil and of dream
> The appointed hour comes;
> Blessed is each day with its cares,
> Blessed is the coming of darkness.

Lensky perceives this but cannot accept it, and his anguished call may not be to Olga, his Muse, but to an unnamed 'desired friend'.

Critical controversy surrounds the character of Onegin. The 19th-century critic Vissarion Belinsky wrote:

> The hero of the poem, Onegin, is a man who feels his superiority over the crowd, who born with great strength of soul is at thirty already dispirited, spent, aloof from all interests, yet unable to settle into the rut of day-to-day living. In the end he will be revived to life for desire will be revived within him, but only because it cannot be fulfilled — and the novel ends in nothing.

In his Pushkin Address, Dostoevsky characterizes Onegin as an aimless wanderer through his native land:

> You see, Tatyana *does* understand who he is. An eternal wanderer suddenly saw a woman, on whom he had once looked down, in new, splendid surroundings. 'This is my ideal,' he exclaims, 'here is my salvation, here is the outcome of my anguished boredom. I passed it by, and happiness was so possible, so near.' He aspires to Tatyana, strives for her, seeking his deliverance in a new, fantastic dream. Cannot Tatyana see this in him, has she not long ago understood him? She knows with certainty that in reality he is in love with his new fantasy, not with her, the Tatyana humble as before! She knows that he is taking her for someone else, not for who she really is, even that he does not love her, that perhaps he does not love anyone, nor is even able to love anyone, although he is tormented so by his sufferings.

In his libretto, Tchaikovsky advances the motif of Onegin's dreams and desires, and his inability to live them and bring them to reality. Onegin scorns Lensky's dream; he confesses to Tatyana that life with her would be a burden to him; and even on his return to St Peterburg he feels his love for Tatyana 'as in a dream'. He states that he will be filled with 'the unrealizable dream of his love' and that 'This is again my dream! That is bliss!' Neither Pushkin nor Tchaikovsky passes judgement on Onegin, nor resolves his torment. Consolation (if not salvation) for Onegin's suffering comes in Tatyana's 'I love you', in her all-forgiving love.

Belinsky's and Dostoevsky's pessimism aside, the theme of a man enraptured by a dream develops across the whole of Pushkin's work, and ends on an optimistic note. In *The Prisoner of the Caucasus* and in *The Gypsies* the hero flees civilization to realize his dream. *Onegin* followed these works, and then, two years before his death, Pushkin wrote 'The Pilgrim', a poem inspired by Bunyan, in which he describes not an aimless wanderer, as in *Onegin*, but a

Larissa Shevchenko and Vladimir Chernov with the Kirov Opera (photos: The Kirov Opera)

pilgrim who has left all for the sake of a love 'not of this world'. Could this possibly have been Onegin's fate as well?

While Onegin as a character may be elusive, Tatyana is simple in her spirituality. She is like the flame of a candle, quivering and flickering in the first windrush of love. Here Tchaikovsky beautifully conveys the emotion of one who could abandon all for passion, or could be guided by the love of family and humility of faith taught her by her nurse. Tchaikovsky insisted that the letter scene be performed complete, including Tatyana's conversation with the nurse, so that we clearly understand the source of the girl's beliefs.

Monsieur Triquet, in the old tradition of a nameday panegyric, sings of Tatyana's spiritual beauty, as yet unrecognised by the others, and wishes her flame to shine forever. The words of Prince Gremin (partially taken from Pushkin's text and partially written by Tchaikovsky) pick up this theme of Tatyana's inner radiance:

> Onegin, I cannot conceal
> How much I love Tatyana,
> Sadly my life flowed, languishing,
> She came and brightened it
> As a ray of sunshine amidst the darkness.
>
> She shines as a star
> On a dark night in a clear sky
> And appears to me always
> In the radiance of an angel,
> The resplendent radiance of an angel!

Tchaikovsky's words are consonant in image and metre with Pushkin's words in the last chapter of the poem:

> There, in mysterious valleys
> In the springtime, at the cries of swans
> Near the waters, radiant in the stillness
> The Muse began to appear to me.

The similarity of metre and rhythm may be observed by aligning the two texts above one another. Especially telling is the way Tatyana's name coincides with Pushkin's word for swans (*lebedinykh*), a symbol of dreams and ideals in Russian song:

O -	né-	gin	yá	skri-	vát'	ne	stá-	nu,
V te	dní	v	táin-	stven-	nykh	do-	- li-	nakh,
Bez-	úm-	no	yá	lyu-	blyú	Ta-	tyá-	nu,
Ves-	nói	pri	klí	kakh	le -	be-	dí-	nykh,
Tosk-	lí-	vo	zhízn'	mo-	yá	te-	klá,
Bliz	vód	si-	yáv-	shikh	v ti-	shi-	né,
O -	ná,	ya -	ví-	las'	i	za-	zhglá.
Yav-	lyát-	sya	Mú-	za	stá-	la	mné.

Tatyana in her steadfast love becomes the symbol for Pushkin and Tchaikovsky of the reality of their music. Tchaikovsky wrote:

> Music is not an illusion, it is a revelation. And in precisely this lies its victorious strength: thus it opens, reveals to us that which is

Galina Vishnevskaya as Tatyana in her debut at the Bolshoi in 1953.

inaccessible in any other sphere, elements of beauty, the contemplation of which is not temporary, but forever reconciles us with life. It spiritually enlightens and rejoices us.

In the end all great art is a commentary on our wanderings, our pilgrimage to the realization of our dreams. Yet there would be no commentary without inspiration, which comes on the one hand from the Artist's Muse, and on the other from us, the audience, of whom a certain compassion is expected. In *Onegin*, Tchaikovsky asks us for that compassion in 'The Singer', the duet the girls are performing as the curtain rises on Act One. Just as Prospero asks his audience to accept his project and his art, so Tchaikovsky asks us to receive the work he offers us without preconceptions, and with affection.

Note: All the translations are the author's.

Galina Vishnevskaya's farewell performance as Tatyana at the Paris Opéra in 1982 (photo: Daniel Cande)

Thematic Guide

Many of the themes from the opera have been identified in the articles by numbers in square brackets, which refer to the themes set out on these pages. The themes are also identified by the numbers in square brackets at the corresponding points in the libretto, so that the words can be related to the musical themes.

[1a]
Tatyana's theme
(used throughout the first act and once in the final scene)
Andante con moto

[1b]
Expanded variant of Tatyana's theme
Andante

[2]
No. 1 Duet of Tatyana and Olga
Andante con moto TATYANA

'Oh, did you hear   the love-sick shep-herd boy'
Sly-kha-li   l'vy   za rosh-chei glas noch-noi

[3]
No. 2 First peasant chorus (protyazhnaya pesnya)
Adagio   CHORUS

My   legs   ache and can no long-er run, now the day is done; —
Bo - lyat   mo- i   sko-ry no-zhen'ki, so po-ko-dush-ki!——

[4]
No. 2 Second peasant chorus (khorovod)
CHORUS
Moderato assai

In   a   cot-tage by the wa-ter
Uzh, kak po mos-tu, mos-toch-ku.

[5]
No. 3 Olga's aria
Andante mosso OLGA

I'm not the sort to   sit   in si - lence;
Ya ne spo-so - bna k grusti tom-noi.

[6]

*No. 6 Lensky's arioso (Variants of this phrase return at the beginning
of the finale of Act Two, Scene One, and in the moments before the duel.)*

Moderato – *with passionate ardour*

I ⸻ love you, I a - dore you, Ol-ga,
Ya lyu - blyu vas, ya lyu - blyu vas, Ol' ga,

[7]

Onegin's theme, Act One, Scene One

Moderato

Do you not find it ra-ther bo-ring li-ving so
Ya du-ma-ya,by va et vam pres-ku-chno zdes'

[8]

from No. 8: 'Tatyana alone'

Andante mosso

[9]

from No. 8: the Nurse's theme

Moderato assai

[10]

from No. 8

Moderato

Oh, Nan- ny, Nan-ny, I'm so wret - ched
Ach, nya - nya, nya-nya, ya stra da - yu

[11]

*from No. 9: Tatyana's first line in the Letter Scene
(sung by Onegin in Act Three)*

[Andante con moto]   Allegro non troppo

To write is fool-ish - ness, I know it, but as I
Pu-skai po - gi-bnu ya, no pre-zhde ya vos-le

love him, I must show it;
pi - tel noi na - dez-hde

[12]

from No. 9: Tatyana begins to write

Moderato assai, quasi Andante

[13]

from No. 9: Tatyana pledges herself to Onegin

Moderato

TATYANA

No, there could ne-ver be an - oth - er to whom I'd give my love!
Net, ni - ko - mu na sve-te ne ot-da - la by serd tsa ya!

[14]

from No. 9

Andante

TATYANA *with great feeling*

Are you an an-gel sent to guard me?
Kto ty, moi an-gel li khra- hi - tel'

[15]

from No. 10: Shepherds' pipes

Allegro moderato

[16]

from No. 10

[Allegro moderato] Poco meno mosso

TATYANA

Then make your grand-son go in sec-ret to take this note to him
I - tak, po-shli ti-khon'ko vnu-ka s za-pis - koi e - toi k O...

[17]

No. 11

[Allegro moderato]

GIRLS' CHORUS

Dear com-pan-ions, come this way, join us in the games we play.
De - vit sy, kra - sa - vi - tsy, du shen'ki po - dru -zhen 'ki!

[18]

from No. 12

Andante non troppo

ONEGIN

Were I the sort who had in-ten-ded to lead a calm do-mes-tic life;
Kog da by zhizn'do-mash-nim kru-gom ya og - ra-ni-chit'zak-ho-tel,

[19]

from No. 12

[Andante non troppo] Più mosso

f ONEGIN

My soul was des-tined to dis - co - ver it sought no o - ther;
Mech-tam i go- dam net vos-vra - ta akh, net vos - vra-ta!

[20]

No. 13: Choral waltz

Tempo di valse

f

[21]

No. 14: theme of Triquet's couplets
[Andantino]

[22]

No. 15: Cotillion (mazurka)
[Tempo di mazurka]

[23]
No. 16: Finale
Andante, with great feeling
LENSKY

It was   here in these peace-ful sur - round - ings   that my
V ra-shem   do - mye, kak sni   zo - lo - ti -   ye,   mo - i

lei - sure was spent as   a   child;
dye - tski - ye   go - di tyek - li!

[24]
No. 17: Act Two, Scene Two, orchestral introduction
Andante

[25]
No. 17: Aria
Andante, quasi Adagio
LENSKY *a piena voce*

Shall I   sur - vive the day that's dawn-ing?
Chto den' gryad-ush-chii mne go -   to - vit?

[26]
Duet of Onegin and Lensky before the duel (Act Two, Scene Two)
[Allegro moderato]

We   fight   to sat - is - fy our   ho - nour
Vra   gi!   Da-vno li drug ot   dru - ga

[27]
No. 19: Polonaise
[moderato, Tempo di polacca]

50

[28]

Tatyana's entrance music, Act Three, Scene One

[Allegro moderato]

[29]

No. 20a: Aria

Andante sostenuto

PRINCE GREMIN

The gift of love is right-ly trea-sured
Lyu - bvi vse vos-ras - ty po - kor - ny

[30]

from No. 22

Andantino

TATYANA

O - ne - gin, I was then far youn-ger,
O - ne - gin, ya to-gda mo - to-zhe,

[31]

from No. 22

Andante molto mosso

TATYANA *con anima*

O-ne - gin as a man of ho-nour you will sure-ly grant my wish!
O-ne - gin vvas hem serdtse est'i gor dost'i prya ma ya chest'

51

Frederick Sharp in the title role at Sadler's Wells in 1952 (photo: Angus McBean © Harvard Theatre Collection)

Eugene Onegin

Lyric Scenes
in three Acts and seven Scenes
by Pyotr Tchaikovsky

Libretto by Konstantin Shilovsky and Pyotr Tchaikovsky,
based on Alexander Pushkin's novel in verse

English version by David Lloyd-Jones

Eugene Onegin was first performed by students of the Conservatory of Music at the Malyi Theatre, Moscow, on March 29, 1879. The professional première was at the Bolshoi Theatre, Moscow on January 23, 1881. The first performance in Britain was given by the Moody-Manners Company at the Olympic Theatre, London, on October 17, 1892, in English. It was first performed at Covent Garden on June 29, 1906 (in Italian). The first performance in the USA was a concert in New York in English on February 1, 1908; the first performance at the Metropolitan Opera was on March 24, 1920.

CHARACTERS

Madame Larina *a widowed landowner*   *mezzo-soprano*
Tatyana *daughter of Madame Larina*   *soprano*
Olga *daughter of Madame Larina*   *contralto*
Filippyevna *an old nurse*   *mezzo-soprano*
Eugene (Yevgeny) Onegin   *baritone*
Vladimir Lensky *a poet*   *tenor*
Prince Gremin *a retired general*   *bass*
A captain   *bass*
Zaretsky *a retired officer*   *bass*
Monsieur Triquet *a Frenchman*   *tenor*
Guillot *Onegin's valet*

Peasants, Guests of Madame Larina, guests at a ball in St Petersburg, Officers.

The action takes place in Russia in the 1820s; Acts One and Two in the country and Act Three in St Petersburg.

Act One, Scene Two in the 1978 Welsh National Opera production by Andrei Serban, designed by Michael Yeargan.

The Russian text is the libretto in the fourth volume of the Complete Collected Works, published in Moscow in 1948. In that edition the most valuable guides to the definitive text were said to be the manuscripts of the full score and the piano score, and the published score with the composer's own notes and alterations. It has been transliterated here to approximate as closely as possible to the sound of the original.

In the preface to the 1948 edition, the editor Ivan Shishov had this to say about the authorship of the libretto:

> The libretto and scenario of the opera were written by P.I. Tchaikovsky in collaboration with his friend K.S. Shilovsky, an actor at the Malyi Theatre in Moscow. N.D. Kashkin recounts in his memoirs of Tchaikovsky how Shilovsky became a collaborator in writing the libretto and how Tchaikovsky often visited him at his estate 'Glebovo' near New Jerusalem. Which portion of the libretto was Shilovsky's, Kashkin did not know exactly. He only knew that the French text of Triquet's couplets was written last.

> From Shilovsky's letter to Tchaikovsky of March 22/10, 1878, we know that Shilovsky asked Tchaikovsky not to attach his name to the printed libretto of *Eugene Onegin*. If Tchaikovsky did not wish to take the responsibility for the libretto on himself, Shilovsky suggested using the initials K.S.Sh, but no more, or his psuedonym 'K. Glebovsky'. In a letter to Shilovsky on May 27/15, 1879, Tchaikovsky thanked him for the vital help he had given in connection with *Eugene Onegin*.

> From this it is clear that Shilovsky's participation was not confined merely to the text of the Triquet couplets, which Kashkin mentions. The reason for Shilovsky's refusal to publish his name as co-author points to a number of disagreements between the authors over the definitive text, concerning the changes and additions to Pushkin's novel.

David Lloyd-Jones's text is a performing version, not a literal translation. The stage directions are those in the libretto, which are fuller than those in the piano score; similarly the punctuation and the lay-out follow the libretto. The numbers in square brackets refer to the Thematic Guide.

Kiri te Kanawa as Tatyana and Gillian Knight as Olga, Covent Garden, 1976 (photo: Donald Southern)

Act One

Introduction [1a]

Scene One. *The garden of the Larin country estate. On the left, a house with a terrace; on the right, a shady tree with a flower-bed nearby. In the background, a dilapidated wooden fence beyond which the village and church are visible through the thick foliage. It is early evening. Madame Larina sits under the tree making jam; Filippyevna is standing near her and helping. The doors leading from the house onto the terrace are open, and singing can be heard coming from within.*

No. 1 Duet and Quartet.

TATYANA & OLGA

'Oh, did you hear the lovesick shepherd boy
Who sings of woe and misery undying?
The morning silence echoes with his sighing
As he pours out his plaintive song of love.

And did you sigh to hear its melody,
His song of love and sadness never-ending,
And see his grief, all other grief transcending,
As in distress he vowed that he would die?'

[2] 'Slykhali l' vy za roshchei glas nochnoi

Pevtsa lyubvi, pevtsa svoei pechali?
Kogda polya v chas utrenii molchali,

Svireli zvuk — unylyi i prostoi.

[1a]
[2] Vzdokhnuli l' vy, vnimaya tikhii glas
Pevtsa lyubvi, pevtsa svoei pechali?

Kogda v lesakh vy yunoshu vidali,

Vstrechaya vzor evo potukhshikh glaz.

The following conversation takes place during the second verse of the girls' song.

MADAME LARINA

I know that song and I remember
How in those long-forgotten days
When I was young, I also sang it.

Oni poyut . . . i ya, byvalo,
V davno proshedshie goda —
Ty pomnysh' li — i ya pevala!

NURSE

Ah, that was many years ago.

Vy byli molody togda!

MADAME LARINA

How I adored those English novels!

Kak ya lyubila Richardsona!

NURSE

Yes, that was many years ago.

Vy byli molody togda!

MADAME LARINA

Not that I read them for myself.
No, it was just because my cousin —
Princess Aline who lived in Moscow —
Would talk of Richardson all day.
Ah, Grandison! Ah, Richardson!

Ne potomu, chtoby prochla,
No v starinu knyazhna Alina,
Moya moskovskaya kuzina,
Tverdila chasto mne o nyom
Akh, Grandison! Akh, Richardson!

NURSE

Yes, I remember.
You'd only just become engaged!
But I knew it wasn't a love-match!
For you had set your heart on someone
More romantically inclined,
And dreamt you might elope together.

Da pomnyu, pomnyu!
V to vremya byl eshchyo zhenikh
Suprug vash . . . No vy ponevole
Togda mechtali o drugom,
Kotoryi serdtsem i umom
Vam nravilsya gorazdo bole.

MADAME LARINA

Ah, so I had! Ah, so I had!
He took my heart away,
That dashing ensign in the Guards!

Akh, Grandison! Akh, Richardson!
Ved' on byl slavnyi frant,
Igrok i gvardii serzhant!

NURSE

It all seems many years ago.

Davno proshedshie goda!

57

MADAME LARINA

I was so elegant in those days . . .	Kak ya vsegda byla odeta!

NURSE

Yes, you looked lovely . . .	Vsegda po mode!

MADAME LARINA

And wore each fashion *à la mode*.	Vsegda po mode i k litsu.

NURSE

. . . And wore each fashion of the day.	Vsegda po mode i k litsu.

MADAME LARINA

But father chose a husband for me.	No vdrug, bez moevo soveta . . .

NURSE

Then you were married straight away;	Svezli vnezapno vas k ventsu.
No wonder you were so unhappy.	Potom, chtoby rasseyat' gore,
But soon you said goodbye to Moscow;	Syuda priekhal barin vskore.
Your noble master brought you here,	Vy tut khozyaistvom zanyalis,
And when your household duties started	Privykli — i dovolnyi stali
You grew contented.	I slava bogu!

MADAME LARINA

At first I woke each morning crying,	Akh, kak ya plakala snachala!
And even longed to run away.	S suprugom chut' ne razvelas'!
But household duties soon began	Potom khozyaistvom zanyalas',
And gradually I grew contented.	Privykla — i dovol'na stala.

The off-stage singing of the girls ends.

MADAME LARINA & NURSE

God sends us habit from above	Privychka svyshe nam dana —
In place of happiness and love.	Zamena schastiyu ona.
The proverb's true!	Da, tak-to, tak!

MADAME LARINA

And so romance, Princess Pauline,	Korset, al'bom, knyazhnu Polinu,
And books of sentimental verse	Stikhov chuvstvitel'nykh tetrad',
Were all forgotten.	Ya vsyo zabyla . . .

NURSE

And you soon preferred to dress in something simpler;	Stali zvat' Akul'koi prezhnyuyu Selinu,
Instead of crinoline and wrap . . .	I obnovili, nakonets . . .

MADAME LARINA & NURSE

Ah! I/you wear a quilted gown and cap.	Akh! Na vate shlafrok i chepets.
God sends us habit from above	Privychka s vyshe nam dana —
In place of happiness and love.	Zamena schastiyu ona.
The proverb's true!	Da, tak-to, tak!

MADAME LARINA

And yet my husband loved me blindly	No muzh menya lyubil serdechno,
And always treated me so kindly.	Vo vsyom mne veroval on bespechno.

NURSE

And yet the master loved you blindly	Da, barin vas lyubil serdechno,
And always treated you so kindly.	Vo vsyom vam veroval bespechno.

MADAME LARINA & NURSE

Yes, God is good, he knows what's best, And all who trust in him surely will find rest.	Privychka svyshe nam dana — Zamena schastiyu ona.

58

The singing of peasants is heard off-stage, gradually coming nearer.

No. 2 Chorus and Dance of the Peasants.

LEADER

My legs ache and can no longer run	[3] Bolyat moi skory nozhen'ki
Now the day is done.	So pokhodushki.

PEASANTS

My poor legs are aching and cannot run.	Skory nozhen'ki so pokhodushki.

LEADER

My hands both are sore from binding corn	Bolyat moi bely ruchen'ki
Since the break of morn.	So rabotushki.

PEASANTS

My poor hands are aching from binding corn.	Bely ruchen'ki so rabotushki.
My heart is grieving from bitter sorrow	Shchemit moyo retivoe serdtse
And never-ending care;	So zabotushki:
My spirit is sore	Ne znayu, kak byt',
For I'll see my love no more.	Kak lyubesnovo zabyt'.

The peasants enter, carrying before them a decorated sheaf of corn.

Health and wealth to your ladyship,	Zdravtsvui, matushka-barynya!
Years of plenty and fellowship!	Zdravstvui, nasha kormilitsa!
Doubtless you know why we come to you	Vot my prishli k tvoei milosti,
Bearing a sheaf as we always do;	Snop prinesli razukrashennyi:
The harvest is finished at last!	S zhatvoi pokonchili my!

MADAME LARINA

Thank you, good people. I'm delighted.	Shto zh, i prekrasno! Veselites'!
You're welcome here.	Ya rada vam!
Let's celebrate the harvest with a song!	Propoite chto-nibud' poveselei!

PEASANTS

Why, that's a pleasure, ma'am.	Izvol'te, matushka!
Sing for her ladyship,	Poteshim barynyu!
And take your places, dancers.	Nu, devki, v krug skhodites'
Come on now, are you ready?	Nu, chto zh vy? Stanovites!

During the song the girls dance with the sheaf and Tatyana and Olga come out onto the balcony.

In a cottage by the water * [4]	Uzh kak po mostu-mostochku.
Lived a miller with his daughter.	Po kalinovym dosochkam —
Fa la la la etc.,	Vainu, vainu, vainu, vainu,
Lived a miller with his daughter.	Po kalinovym dosochkam.
Came a farmer on the ferry,	Tut i shyol, proshyol detina —
Rich and ruddy as a cherry.	Slovno yagoda-malina,
Fa la la la etc.,	Vainu, vainu, vainu, vainu,
Rich and ruddy as a cherry.	Slovna yagoda-malina.
Saw the miller's pretty daughter,	Na pleche nesyot dubinku,
Started then and there to court her.	Pod poloi nesyot volynku,
Fa la la la etc.,	Vainu, vainu, vainu, vainu,
Started then and there to court her.	Pod poloi nesyot volinku.
Thought he'd manage to persuade her	Pod drugoi nesyot gudochek,
If he came to serenade her.	Dogadaisya, mil-druzhochek!
Fa la la la etc.,	Vainu, vainu, vainu, vainu,
If he came to serenade her.	Dogadaisya, mil-druzhochek!

---

* A closer translation would be: 'Across the little bridge, across its wooden planks, pa' youth, ruddy as a raspberry. A stout stick on his shoulder, a bag-pipe beneath his whistle on the other side. Guess, my little dear one! The sun has set. Are you st' Come out yourself, send someone else, send Sasha, or send Masha, or litt' Pareshenka came out, talked to her sweetheart: Do not scold me, little friend, I was, in a thin and very short nightshirt.'

'Won't you listen to my pleading?
I'm a gentleman of breeding.'
Fa la la la etc.,
'I'm a gentleman of breeding.'

'Solntse selo. Ty ne spish' li?
Libo vyidi, libo vyshli — '
Vainu, vainu, vainu, vainu,
'Libo vyidi, libo vyshli.'

'You have said the same to Sasha;
Broke your promise to Parasha!'
Fa la la la etc.,
'Broke your promise to Parasha!'

'Libo Sashu, libo Mashu,
Libo dushechku Parashu,'
Vainu, vainu, vainu, vainu,
'Libo dushechku Parashu.'

'Don't believe that harridan Parasha,
When I see her next I swear I'll thrash her!
Don't believe Parasha,
Who's been gossiping with Masha;
If we meet again I'll thrash her!'

Sashu, libo dushechku Parashu,
Libo Sashu, libo Mashu,

Libo dushechku, Parashu,
Libo Sashu, libo Mashu
Libo dushechku Parashu!

But the miller's pretty daughter
Shouted back across the water,
Fa la la la etc.,
Shouted back across the water.

Parashen'ka vykhodila
S milym rechi govorila
Vainu, vainu, vainu, vainu,
S milym rechi govorila.

'Though you've got your fascination,
I must keep my reputation,
So I'll be at your disposal
When you make me a proposal!'

Ne bessud'ka, moi druzhochek,
V chyom khodila, v tom i vyshla,
V khuden' koi vo rubashonke,
Vo korotkoi ponizhonke.

Fa la la la etc.!

Vainu, vainu, vainu, vainu!

No. 3 Scene and Aria.

TATYANA
(with book in hand)

Oh, how I love to hear the people singing,
For music makes me lose myself
In endless yearning for something far away!

[16] Kak ya lyublyu pod zvuki pesen etikh
Mechtami unosit'sya inogda kuda-to
Kuda-to daleko . . .

Olga and Tatyana come down from the balcony and join their mother.

OLGA

Ah, Tanya, Tanya, you dream the whole day long!
I'm not like you at all; when I hear songs
They always set me dancing.

Akh, Tanya, Tanya!

Vsegda mechtaesh' ty. A ya tak ne v tebya,
Mne veselo, kogda ya pen'e slyshu.

She dances.

'In a cottage by the water
Lived a miller with his daughter.'

[4] Uzh kak po mostu-mostochku,
Po kalinovym dosochkam ! ! !

Olga embraces her mother and then moves down-stage to sing. Madame Larina, the Nurse and Tatyana gather round her.

I'm not the sort to sit in silence,
At night I never stay awake
And watch the moonlight at my window,
Or sigh and sigh and sigh
As if my heart would break!

[5] Ya ne sposobna k grusti tomnoi,
Ya ne lyublyu mechtat' v tishi,
Il' na balkone noch'yu tyomnoi

Vzdykhat', vzdykhat',
Vzdykhat' iz glubiny dushi.

So why be sad? Behave as I do
And lead a life that's always gay;
For when you're cheerful and fond of laughter
The heart grows younger every day.
Never give way to sorrow or despair;
Each morning calls anew to pleasure!
My love of life's beyond all measure,
That's why my fancy's free of care!

Zachem vzdykhat', kogda schastlivo
Moi dni yunye tekut?
Ya bezzabotna i shalovliva,

Menya rebyonkom vse zovut!
Mne budet zhizn' vsegda mila,
I ya ostanus', kak i prezhde,
Podobno vetrenoi nadezhde,
Rezva, bespechna, vesela!

60

No. 4 Scene.

MADAME LARINA
(to Olga)

Come here, my darling Olga!	Nu ty, moya vostrushka,
I love to see you happy and contented.	Vesyolaya i rezvaya ty ptashka!
You'd really like to spend the whole day dancing,	Ya dumayu — plyasat' seichas gotova,
I'm sure of it!	Ne pravda li?

Tatyana and the Nurse walk away from the others.

NURSE

Tanyusha, what's the matter? Tell me, child;	[9] Tanyusha! A Tanyusha! Chto s toboi?
Perhaps you're feeling ill.	Uzh ne bol'na li ty?

TATYANA

No, Nanny, please don't worry.	[1a] Net, Nyanya, — ya zdorova.

MADAME LARINA
(turning to the peasants)
[4]

Good people, let me thank you for your singing.	Nu, milye, spasibo vam za pesni!
You must be thirsty now.	Stupaite k fligelyu. Filipp'evna,
Filippyevna, arrange for wine before they leave.	A ty veli im dat' vina.
My friends, God bless you!	Proshchaite, drugi!

PEASANTS

Goodbye, and thank you, ma'am!	Proshchaite, matushka!
[4]	

The Nurse goes out with the peasants. Tatyana sits down on the terrace steps and becomes engrossed in her book.

OLGA

Oh, mother, what's the matter with Tatyana?	Mamasha, posmotrite-ka na Tanyu!

MADAME LARINA

Dear, dear! Indeed, you look quite pale, my darling.	A chto? I vpryam' moi drug, bledna ty ochen'!

TATYANA

But no more than usual,	Ya vsegda takaya, —
You're far too anxious, mother!	Vy ne trevozh'tes', mama!
Can't you see I'm busy reading my novel?	Ochen', interesno to, chto chitayu.

MADAME LARINA
(laughing)

Ah, clearly that's the reason!	Tak ottogo bledna ty?

TATYANA

It's such a moving tale of two young people;	[1b] Da kak zhe, mama; povest' muk serdechnykh
They're both in love yet so unhappy	Vlublyonnykh dvukh menya volnuet
And I'm sorry for them.	Mne tak zhal' ikh, bednykh!
Oh, how they had to suffer!	Akh, kak oni stradayut!

MADAME LARINA

Tanya darling, when I was young I too	Polno, Tanya! Byvalo, ya, kak ty,
Would get upset from reading these romances.	Chitaya knigi eti, volnovalas'
They're all made up, my child!	Vsyo eto vymysel! Proshli goda,

As time went by I came to realise that in life
There are no heroes or heroines.

I ya uvidela, chto v zhizni net geroev.

Pokoina ya . . .

OLGA

You try to sound so worldly but all the time
Forget you've got your apron on!
Think what a sight you'd look if Lensky came!

Naprasno tak pokoiny!

Smotrite: fartuk vash vy snyat' zabyli!
Nu, kak priedet Lensky — chto togda?

Olga laughs; Madame Larina hastily takes off her apron.

Hush, there's a carriage coming!
Here he is!

[1a] Chu! Podezzhaet kto-to . . .
Eto on!

MADAME LARINA

What, here already!

I v samom dele!

TATYANA
(looking down from the terrace)

He's not alone.

On ne odin . . .

MADAME LARINA

Who can it be?

Kto b eto byl?

The Nurse enters in haste with a coachman.

NURSE

Excuse me, ma'am, he says it's Mister Lensky;
Mister Onegin's with him.

[1a] Sudarynya, priekhal Lensky barin,

S nim gospodin Onegin!

TATYANA

Oh, in that case I must go!

Akh! Skoree ubegu! . . .

She wants to run away; Madame Larina restrains her.

MADAME LARINA

What nonsense, Tanya! They'll be offended.
Heavens above! My cap is on all askew!

Kuda ty, Tanya? Tebya osudyat! . . .

Batyushki, a chepchik moi na boku! . . .

The Nurse arranges Tatyana's dress and then goes out, motioning her not to be afraid.

OLGA
(to Madame Larina)

Why don't you ask them in?

Velite zhe prosit'!

MADAME LARINA
(to the coachman)

Invite them in at once!

Prosi skorei, prosi!

The coachman runs out. In great excitement they all prepare to receive the guests. Enter Onegin and Lensky. Lensky goes up to Madame Larina, kisses her hand and bows to the girls courteously.

No. 5 Scene and Quartet.

LENSKY

Mesdames, I hope that you'll excuse me,
I've brought a visitor; this is Onegin,
My neighbour and my friend.

Mesdames! Ya na sebya vzyal smelost'
Privest' priyatelya. Rekomenduyu vam:
Onegin, moi sosed.

ONEGIN

I'm greatly honoured.

Ya ochen' schastliv!

MADAME LARINA
(flustered)

No really, sir, it's we who are honoured.
Be seated and meet my daughters.

Pomiluite, my rady vam; prisyad'te!
Vot docheri moi.

62

ONEGIN

I find them charming, ma'am.	Ya ochen', ochen' rad!

MADAME LARINA

Let's go inside to talk,	Voidyomte v komnaty! Il' mozhet byt', khotite
Or, if you would prefer it,	Na vol'nom vozdukhe ostat'sya?
We could remain here in the garden.	Proshu vas, —
I beg you, don't stand on ceremony;	Bez tseremonii bud'te: my sosedi, —
We are neighbours, so do exactly as you please.	Tak nam chinit'sya nechevo!

LENSKY
(to Onegin)

I love it here! There's nowhere else that's quite so peaceful	Prelestno zdes'! Lyublyu ya etot sad,
Or secluded. It's just delightful!	Ukromnyi i tenistyi! V nyom tak uyutno!

MADAME LARINA

Stay here then!	Prekrasno!
But I must go indoors to see about the supper.	Poidu pokhlopotat' ya v dome po khozyaistvu.
My girls will entertain you. A bientôt!	A vy gostei zaimite. Ya seichas!

She goes out, motioning Tatyana not to be shy. Lensky and Onegin walk over to the right. Tatyana and Olga stand on the opposite side.

ONEGIN
(to Lensky)

Now tell me, which of them's Tatyana?	Skazhi, kotoraya Tatiana,
I'm really interested to know.	Mne ochen' lyubopytno znat'.

LENSKY

The older one who's looking sad,	Da ta, kotoraya grustna
With eyes cast downwards so demurely.	I molchaliva, kak Svetlana.

ONEGIN

I'm most surprised you've chosen Olga.	Neuzhto ty vlyublen v men'shuyu?

LENSKY

And why?	A chto?

ONEGIN

For I'd prefer the other	Ya vybral by druguyu,
Were I a poet just like you.	Kogda b ya byl, kak ty, poet.
Your Olga seems to have no fire,	V chertakh u Ol'gi zhizni net,
No special character or passion.	Toch'-v-toch' v Vandikovoi Madone:
I'll grant she has a pretty face,	Krugla, krasna litsom ona,
But like the moon it lacks all grace;	Kak eta glupaya luna na etom glupom nebosklone.
Yes, like the moon it's vacant and prosaic.	Ya vybral by druguyu.

LENSKY

Clearly there is a gulf between us;	Akh, milyi drug, volna i kamen',
For prose and verse	Stikhi i prosa, lyod i plamen'
Or fire and water	Ne stol' razlichny mezh soboi,
Aren't more unlike than you and I!	Kak my vsaimnoi raznotoi!

TATYANA
(to herself)

Now, now at last my eyes are open,	Ya dozhdalas', otkrylis' ochi!
My heart assures me it is he!	Ya znayu, znayu: eto on!
And now I know his precious image	Uvy, teper' dni, i nochi,
Will haunt me for the rest of life.	I zharkii odinokii son, —
I'll dream each night of my beloved.	Vsyo, vsyo napolnit obraz milyi!

His coming has aroused within me
The magic feeling of desire,
And set my loving soul on fire.

Bez umolku volshebnoi siloi
Vsyo budet mne tverdit' o nyom
I dushu zhech' lyubvi ognyom!

OLGA
(to herself)

I always knew that when Onegin came
here
His elegance and easy social grace
Would make a deep impression.
The gossips will begin to talk
And make their scandalous conclusions.
Slyly, they'll call him eligible
Though also hint that he's depraved.
The village gossips now will start to
whisper
And link Tatyana's name with his.

Akh, znala ya, chto poyavlen'e
Onegina proizvedyot
Na vsekh bol'shoe vpechatlen'e
I vsekh sosedei razvlechyot:
Poidet dogadka za dogadkoi,
Vse stanut tolkovat' ukradkoi,
Poidet dogadka za dogadkoi,
Shutit', sudit' ne bez grekha!
I Tane prochit' zhenikha!

Lensky goes up to Olga. Onegin looks nonchalantly at Tatyana who stands with downcast eyes. He then goes up to her and engages her in conversation.

No. 6 Scene and Arioso.

LENSKY
(ardently, to Olga)

How perfect, how wonderful,
To be once more together!

[6] Kak schastliv ya, kak schastliv ya:
Ya snova vizhus' s vami!

OLGA

I thought we met here only yesterday.

Vchera my videlis', mne kazhetsya?

LENSKY

I know, but that was ages.
One whole day of separation —
It seemed endless!

O da! No vsyo zh den' tselyi,
Dolgii den' proshol v rasluke.
Eto vechnost'!

OLGA

Endless! You make it sound so terrible!
Don't exaggerate!

[6] Vechnost'! Kakoe slovo strashnoe!
Vechnost' — den' odin!

LENSKY

The word was strong, Olga,
Even as my love for you!

Da, slovo strashnoe,
No ne dlya moei lyubvi!

Lensky and Olga walk away. Onegin and Tatyana come forward. He talks to her with cool politeness.

ONEGIN

But tell me, though,
Do you not find it rather boring
Living so cut off?
It's very quaint but somewhat rustic;
There's nothing here to offer you
Distraction or give amusement.

Skazhite mne, —
[7] Ya dumayu, byvaet vam
Preskuchno zdes', v glushi,
Khotya prelestnoi, no dalyokoi?
Ne dumayu, chtob mnogo razvlechenii
Dano vam bylo.

TATYANA

Well, I'm fond of reading.

[1a] Ya chitayu mnogo.

ONEGIN

Really. It's true that books can give us
pleasure;
I enjoy them also,
But even reading surely has its limits!

[7] Pravda, dayot nam chten'e bezdnu
pishchi
Dlya uma i serdtsa,
No ne vsegda sidet' nam mozhno s
knigoi!

TATYANA

I daydream as I wander through the
garden.

[1a] Mechtayu inogda, brodya po sadu . . .

	ONEGIN
What is it that you dream about?	[1a] O chom zhe vy mechtaete?
	TATYANA
My greatest joy is meditation	Zadumchivost' — moya podruga
And has been since I was a child.	Ot samykh kolybel'nykh dnei.
	ONEGIN
I see that you're incurably romantic;	Ya vizhu — vy mechtatel'nyi uzhasno.
I too once used to be the same.	I ya takim kogda-to byl!

Onegin and Tatyana move away to the opposite side of the garden while Lensky and Olga return.

LENSKY
(to Olga with passionate ardour)

How I love you and adore you, Olga,	[6] Ya lyublyu vas, ya lyublyu vas, Ol'ga,
With the hopeless longing of a poet's fervour,	Kak odna bezumnaya dusha poeta
As only he is doomed to love!	Eshcho lyubit' osuzhdena:
My heart is ruled by one emotion,	Vsegda, vesde odno mechtan'e,
One constant yearning for devotion,	Odno privychnoe zhelan'e
For you're my goddess and my muse.	Odna privychnaya pechal'.
While still a boy my heart was captured;	Ya otrok byl, toboi plenyonnyi,
Your voice would haunt me night and day.	Serdechnykh muk eshcho ne znav
I watched your innocence, enraptured,	Ya byl svidetel' umilyonnyi
And heard you laughing at your play.	Tvoikh mladencheskikh zabav.
We lived not caring for the morrow;	V teni khranitel'noi dubravy
Sharing each childish joy and sorrow.	Ya razdelyal tvoi zabavy. Akh!
Ah!	
How I worship you, how I worship you,	Ya lyublyu tebya, ya lyublyu tebya,
With that hopeless love known only to a poet!	Kak odna dusha poeta tol'ko lyubit:
You are all my inspiration,	Ty odna v moikh mechtan'yakh,
You alone are all my gladness,	Ty odna moyo zhelan'e,
All my happiness and sadness!	Ty mne radost' i stradan'e.
For I love you, I adore you,	Ya lyublyu tebya, ya lyublyu tebya,
And there's no power on earth,	I nikogda nichto:
No time or distance that could keep us both apart,	Ni okhlazhdayushchaya dal'
Or ever cool the ardour	Ni chas razluki, ni vesel'ya shum —
Of my pure desire,	Ne otrezvyat dushi,
For love has warmed it with eternal fire!	Sogretoi devstvennym ognyom lyubvi!

OLGA

Our days of childhood were serene	Pod krovom sel'skoi tishiny
Amid this quiet rural scene.	Rosli s toboyu vmeste my . . .

LENSKY

For I worship you!	Ya lyublyu tebya!

OLGA

Our parents watched us as we grew	I, pomnish', prochili ventsy,
And knew that I would marry you.	Uzh v rannem detstve nam s toboi nashi otsy.

LENSKY

Yes, I worship you and only you!	Ya lyublyu tebya, ya lyublyu tebya!

Madame Larina and the Nurse come out onto the terrace. It grows darker; by the end of the scene it is night.

No 7 Closing Scene.

MADAME LARINA

Ah, here you are! But what's become of Tanya?	A, vot i vy! Kuda zhe delas' Tanya?

She must be with our guest down by the lakeside.
I'll go at once and call her.

Dolzhno byt', u pruda gulyaet s gostem
Poidu eyo poklikat'.

MADAME LARINA

Yes, and say to her
She should be in by now. Our guests are hungry,
And soon it will be supper-time.

Da skazhi-ka ei:
Pora-de v komnaty, gostei golodnykh
Popotchevat' chem bog poslal.

(to Lensky)

So meanwhile, let's go indoors.

Proshu vas, pozhaluite!

LENSKY

We'll follow you, ma'am.

My vsled za vami!

The Nurse goes out. Onegin and Tatyana enter. The Nurse re-enters behind them, trying to over-hear their conversation. Onegin walks calmly across the stage and by the end of his speech has reached the terrace. Tatyana still shows signs of embarrassment.

ONEGIN
(to Tatyana)

My uncle wrote that he was ailing
And so I called on him down here.
Thank God, he died a few weeks later
And earned my gratitude, I fear,
For he had left me quite a fortune!
But, Lord above, I found it tedious
To sit beside him night and day,
Just waiting till he passed away!

[7] Moi dyadya, samykh chestnykh pravil,
Kogda ne v shutku zanemog,
On uvazhat' sebya zastavil,
I luchshe vydumat' ne mog.
Evo primer drugim nauka.
No, bozhe moi, kakaya skuka
S bol'nym sidet' i den' i noch'
Ne otkhodya ni shagu proch'!

They go into the house.

NURSE

My poor Tanyusha! She looks so timid,
Her eyes cast meekly down, and never speaking.
How pale she's looking, and how shy!
Can that young gentleman have caught my darling's fancy?

Moya golubka skloniv golovku
I glazki opustiv, idyot smirnen'ko . . .
Stydliva bol'no! . . . A i to!
Ne priglyanulsya li ei barin etot novyi . . .

She goes off pensively, shaking her head.

Scene Two. *Tatyana's room, very simply furnished with old-fashioned, white wooden chairs covered with chintz, and window curtains of the same material. A bed, over which is a bookshelf. A chest-of-drawers, covered with a cloth and on it, a mirror on a stand. Vases of flowers. At the window, a table with writing materials. As the curtain rises, Tatyana, wearing a white nightdress, is sitting before her mirror very much lost in thought. The Nurse is standing near her.*

No. 8 Introduction and Scene. [8, 1b]

NURSE

There! No more talk tonight.
It's bedtime, Tanya.
You must be up in time for church tomorrow.
Now sleep, my child.

Nu, zaboltalas' ya!
Pora uzh, Tanya! Rano
Tebya ya razbuzhu k obedne.
Zasni skorei.

Tatyana rises listlessly and sits on the bed. The Nurse caresses her. [1b]

TATYANA

I can't sleep, Nanny. It's so sultry.
Open the window and sit by me.

Ne spitsya, nyanya, zdes' tak dushno!
Otkroi okno i syad' ko mne.

The Nurse opens the window and sits on a chair beside Tatyana. [1a]

NURSE

Tanya, what's wrong with you?

Chto, Tanya, chto s toboi?

I'm restless,
So tell me more about the past.

TATYANA

Mne skuchno,
Pogovorim o starine!

NURSE

That's not so easy. In the old days
My head was full of any number
Of fairy stories and old wives' tales,
Of ancient legends and romance.
Today, though, my poor memory's
  failing;
Those tales are quite forgotten.
Ah! My mind grows weaker every day.
Yes, truly!

[9] O chyom zhe, Tanya? Ya, byvalo,
Khranila v pamyat' ne malo
Starinnykh bylei i nebylits
Pro zlykh dukhov i pro devits,
A nyne vsyo temno mne stalo:

Chto znala, to zabyla. Da!
Prishla khudaya chereda!
Zashibla!

[1a]

TATYANA

Tell me something else, then.
When you were just a girl like me,
Did you not fall in love at all?

Rasskazhi mne, nyanya,
Pro vashi starye goda:
Byla ty vlyublena togda?

NURSE

Now really, Tanya! What a question!
No one in those days spoke of love,
And if I'd used that word my husband's
  mother
Would have sent me packing.

I polno, Tanya! V nashi leta
My ne slykhali pro lyubov' —
A to pokoinitsa svekrov'

Menya by sognala so sveta!

[1a]

TATYANA

Then why did you get married, Nanny?

Da kak zhe ty venchalas', nyanya?

NURSE

God willed it so, and so it happened,
When I was just thirteen years old.
Vanya was even younger still.
The match was settled by our parents,
My dowry fixed, and then one day
My father blessed me with a kiss.
I cried, and no one could console me.
Weeping, my friends unbound my braids
And led me solemnly to church.
And so I went to live with strangers . . .
But you're not listening to me, child!

[9] Tak, vidno, bog velel. Moi Vanya
Molozhe byl menya, moi svet,
A bylo mne trinadtsat' let!
Nedeli dve khodila svakha
K moei rodne, i nakonets,
Blagoslovil menya otets!
Ya gor'ko plakala so strakha,
[9] Mne s plachem kosu raspleli,
I s pen'em v tserkov' poveli.
I vot vveli v sem'yu chuzhuyu . . .
Da ty ne slushaesh' menya?

Tatyana embraces the Nurse with passionate emotion.

TATYANA

Oh, Nanny, Nanny, I'm so wretched, so
  unhappy.
I feel like bursting into tears and
  sobbing,
For my heart is bursting.

[10] Akh, nyanya, nyanya, ya stradayu, ya
        tockuyu
Mne toshno, milaya moya

Ya plakat', ya rydat' gotova!

NURSE

There, there, my child, you must be ill.
But God will cure you, you shall see.
Come, let me sprinkle holy water on
  you,
You're all on fire.

Ditya moyo, ty nezdorova;
[9] Gospod' pomilui i spasi!
Dai okroplyu tebya svyatoi vodoi,

Ty vsya gorish' . . .

TATYANA
(hesitantly)

I am not ill;
I'll tell you, Nanny, I'm . . . I'm in love!

[10] Ya ne bol'na,
Ya . . . znaesh' . . . nyanya, ya . . .
        vlyublena!

67

So leave me now, please leave me now,
For I'm in love!

Ostav' menya, ostav' menya ...
Ya vlyublena!

NURSE

But Tanya ...

Da kak zhe ...

TATYANA

I beg you, leave me here alone.
First bring my writing desk and paper,
My pen as well. I'll go to bed then.
Good night!

Podi, ostav' menya odnu.
Dai, nyanya, mne pero, bumagu,
Da stol pridvin', ya skoro lyagu ...
[9] Prosti!

NURSE
(doing what she is told)

Good night! Sleep soundly, Tanya!

Pokoinoi nochi, Tanya!

She goes out.

No. 9 The Letter Scene./Tatyana remains for a long time lost in thought. Then she rises, very agitated
and with an expression of resolute determination. [10]

TATYANA

To write is foolishness, I know it,
But as I love him, I must show it.
And though I suffer evermore,
I'll learn what love may have in store!
Desire has poisoned me with longing;
All day I only think of him.
For though I hide in my despair,
My fatal tempter finds me there;
My tempter haunts my footsteps
   everywhere!

[11] Puskai pogibnu ya, no prezhde
Ya v oslepitel'noi nadezhde
Blazhenstvo tyomnoe zovu,
Ya negu zhizni uznayu!
Ya p'yu volshebnyi yad zhelanii,
Menya presleduyut mechty!
Vezde, vezde peredo mnoi
Moi iskusitel' rokovoi,
Vezde, vezde on predo mnoi! ...

She goes to the writing table, sits down and writes, then pauses. [1b]

No, that won't do! I'll start another.

Net, vsyo ne to! Nachnu snachala! ...

She tears up the letter.

What's wrong with me? I'm all on fire.
I can't think how to start.

Akh, chto so mnoi! Ya vsya goryu!
Ne znayu, kak nachat'!

She writes again, then pauses and reads over what she has written. [12]

'I have to write, my heart compels me;
What is there more that I can say?
For now I know that you'll disdain me
For acting rashly in this way.
But if you'd only show compassion
And think how wretched I must be,
You'll surely not abandon me!
At first I meant to hide my feelings;
Believe me, I had hoped that you would
   never know them;
Never know, never know!'

Ya k vam pishu — chevo zhe bole?
Chto ya mogu eshcho skazat'?
Teper', ya znayu, v vashei vole
Menya prezren'em nakazat'!
No vy, k moei neschastnoi dole
Khot' kaplyu zhalosti khranya,
Vy ne ostavite menya!
Snachala ya molchat' khotela,
Pover'te: moevo styda

Vy ne uznali b nikogda, nikogda!

She lays the letter aside.

Oh, yes, I'd sworn that I would hide my
   love.
And not betray this madness that
   consumes me.
But now I cannot hide my passion any
   more;
Fate has decreed whatever lies in store.

O da, klyalas' ya sokhranit' v dushe

Priznan'e v strasti pylkoi i bezumnoi.

[1a] Uvy! Ne v silakh ya vladet' svoei
   dushoi!
Pust' budet to, chto byt' dolzhno so
   mnoi, —

I shall declare myself and trust in my
   confession!

Emu priznayus' ya! Smelei! On vsyo
   uznaet!

She writes again. [12]

'Whatever brought you to this lonely
   place?
For since we live here in seclusion
I never would have seen your face,
Or known the pangs of bitter torment.

Zachem, zachem vy posetili nas?

V glushi zabytovo selen'ya
Ya b nikogda ne znala vas,
Ne znala b gor'kovo muchen'ya.

68

My heart would soon have grown contented
And then as time went by, who knows,
I might by chance have found another,
Agreed to honour and respect him,
And made a faithful, loving wife...'

She becomes lost in thought, then rises suddenly.

Another! No, there could never be another
To whom I'd give my love!
My life is bound to yours for ever;
This is decreed by heaven above.
Now my existence has a meaning,
Your noble soul for which I sigh.
I know that God above has sent you
To guard and love me till I die!
Often I'd seen you in my dreaming;
Your noble face had long been clear.
Nightly you whispered in my ear;
Your words disturbed me with their meaning.
And then... no, it was not a dream!
For when we met, at once I knew you,
And in that instant, beating wildly,
My heart cried out to me: 'Love him, Love him!'
For you were always there beside me
When, sick at heart, I knelt in prayer.
Your noble presence seemed to guide me
When I would help the poor and Needy in charity.
Yes, it is your beloved vision
That comes in this moment of decision
To stand beside me as I write,
And fill my heart with new emotion,
With whispered promise of devotion
That brings me comfort and delight.

She goes to the table and sits down again to write.

'Are you an angel sent to guard me,
Or will you tempt and then discard me?
Resolve these doubts I can't dispel.
Could all my dreams be self-delusion?
Am I too innocent to tell?
Has fate prepared its own conclusion?'

She again rises and walks about pensively.

'No, come what may, I'm now resolved
To lay my empty life before you.
Pity my burning tears and grant me
Your protection, I implore you,
I implore you!
Believe me, I am all alone;
There's no one here who understands me.

She comes downstage.

I fear my reason will desert me;
To find release I'd gladly die.
I long for you,
Oh, how I long for you to save me;
One word can set my heart on fire
Or simply stifle my desire,
To leave me desolate and wretched!'

She goes quickly to the table and hurriedly finishes the letter. Then she stands up and seals it.

It's finished! Dare I read it through?
For shame and terror now assail me.
But since his honour is my pledge
I boldly trust he will not fail me!

Dushi neopytnoi volnen'ya
Smiriv so vremenem (kak znat'?)
Po serdtsu ya nashla by druga,
Byla by vernaya supruga
I dobrodetel'naya mat'...

[13] Drugoi! Net, nikomu na svete
Ne otdala by serdtsa ya!
To v vyshnem suzhdeno sovete,
To volya neba: ya tvoya!
Vsya zhizn' moya byla zalogom,
Svidan'ya vernovo s toboi;
Ya znayu, ty mne poslan bogom
Do groba ty khranitel' moi!
Ty v snoviden'yakh mne yavlyalsya,
Nezrimyi, ty uzh byl mne mil.
Tvoi chudnyi vzglyad menya tomil,
V dushe tvoi golos razdavalsya!

Davno... Net, eto byl ne son!
Ty chut' voshol, ya vmig uznala,
Vsya obomlela, zapylala,
I v myslyakh molvila: vot on!
Vot on!

[13] Ne pravda l', ya tebya slykhala:
Ty govoril so mnoi v tishi,
Kogda ya bednym pomogala
Ili molitvoi uslazhdala
Tosku dushi?
I v eto samoe mgnoven'e
Ne ty li, miloe viden'e
V prozrachnoi temnote mel'knul,
Proniknul tikho k izgolov'yu,
Ne ty l', s otradoi i lyubov'yu
Slova nadezhdy mne shepnul?

[14] Kto ty, moi angel li khranitel'
Ili kovarnyi iskusitel',
Moi somnen'ya razreshi.
Byt mozhet, eto vsyo pustoe,
Obman neopytnoi dushi,
I suzhdeno sovsem inoe?

[1a] No tak i byt'! Sud'bu moyu
Otnyne ya tebe vruchayu,
Pered toboyu slyozy l'yu,
Tvoei zashchity umolyayu,
Umolyayu.
[14] Voobrazi: ya zdes' odna!
Nikto menya ne ponimaet!

Rassudok moi iznemogaet,
I molcha gibnut' ya dolzhna!
Ya zhdu tebya,
Ya zhda tebya! Edinym slovom
Nadezhdy serdtsa ozhivi,
Il' son tyazholyi perervi,
Uvy, zasluzhennym ukorom!

Konchayu! Strashno perechest',
Stydom i strakhom zamirayu,
No mne porukoi chest' evo,
I smelo ei sebya vveryayu!

No. 10 Scene and Duet.

Tatyana goes to the window and draws the curtains. Daylight quickly fills the room.

Ah, night is over!	Akh, noch' minula,
The rising sun	Prosnulos' vsyo,
Awakes another day.	I solnyshko vstayot ...

She sits by the window. [15]

There goes the shepherd ...	Pastukh igraet,
The world's at peace.	Spokoino vsyo ...
But I'm not, I'm not!	A ya-to, ya-to?

She becomes lost in thought. The door opens quietly and the Nurse enters. At first she does not notice Tatyana. [10]

NURSE

It's time to dress, my dear. Wake up! [9] Pora, ditya moyo! Vstavai!

She sees Tatyana.

Why, what is this? You're up already!	Da ty, krasavitsa, gotova!
You must have risen with the lark.	O, ptashka rannyaya moya!
Last night I feared that you were ill,	Vechor uzh kak boyalas' ya ...
But, thank the Lord, that's over now and done with.	No, slava bogu, ty, ditya, zdorova!
You're quite your cheerful self again.	Toski nochnoi i sledu net,
Your cheeks have got their colour back.	Litso tvoyo — kak makov tsvet!

Tatyana comes from the window and picks up the letter.

TATYANA

Oh, Nanny, may I ask a favour? Akh, nyanya, sdelai odolzhen'e ...

NURSE

Of course, my darling, tell me what. Izvol', rodnaya — prikazhi!

TATYANA

Don't think that ... really ... or suspect that ...	Ne dumai ... pravo ... podozren'e ...
Just promise, *promise* that you'll do it!	No vidish' ... Akh, ne otkazhi!

NURSE

There, there, I'll give my word of honour.	Moi drug, vot bog tebe porukoi.

TATYANA

Then make your grandson go in secret	[16] Itak, poshli tikhon'ko vnuka
To take this note to him — you know —	S zapiskoi etoi k O ... k tomu ...
That gentleman who lives nearby,	K sosedu ... Da veli emu,
And make him promise that he'll never reveal	Chtob on ne govoril ni slova, chtob on,
Who wrote it or from whom it came.	Chtob on ... ne nazyval menya!

NURSE

To whom? I didn't catch the name.	Komu zhe, milaya moya?
I'm growing slow of understanding.	Ya nynche stala bestolkova!
We've got so many neighbours here,	Krugom sosedei mnogo est',
I cannot know them all, I fear.	Kuda mne ikh i perechest';
Speak up, now, and tell me as plainly as you can.	Komu zhe, komu zhe, ty tol'kom govori!

TATYANA
(impatiently)

Nanny, how can you be so stupid! Kak nedogadliva ty, nyanya!

NURSE

My dear, I must be getting old,	Serdechnyi drug, uzh ya stara,
My wits have started to forsake me.	Stara, tupeet pazum, Tanya;
But once they were as bright as gold	A to, byvalo, ya vostra.

And that's why the master put you into my keeping.	Byvalo . . . byvalo . . . mne slovo barskoi voli . . .

TATYANA

Oh, Nanny, what does all that matter? I tell you that my letter is for The neighbour who was here the other day.	[16] Akh, nyanya, nyanya, do tovo li? Chto nuzhdy mne v tvoyom ume, Ty vidish', nyanya, delo o pis'me . . .

NURSE

I understand now.	Nu, delo, delo, delo!

TATYANA

It must be taken to Onegin's house.	Chto nuzhdy, nyanya, mne v tvoyom ume.

NURSE

Please don't be angry that my mind's astray, I'm growing older every day.	Ne gnevaisya, dusha moya, Ty znaesh', neponyatna ya!

TATYANA

Onegin's house!	K Oneginu!

NURSE

I understand now.	Nu, delo, delo!

TATYANA

Onegin's house!	K Oneginu!

NURSE

I understand!	Ya ponyala!

TATYANA

So send your grandson with my letter to Onegin.	S pis'mom k Oneginu poshli ty vnuka, nyanya!

NURSE

Please don't be angry that my mind's astray, I'm growing older every day. But Tanya, why have you turned paler?	Nu, nu, gnevaisya, dusha moya, Ty znaesh', neponyatna ya! Da chto zh ty snova poblednela?

TATYANA

Truly, there's no cause for dismay; Just send your grandson on his way!	Tak, nyanya . . . Pravo, nichevo . . . Poshli zhe nvuka svoevo!

The Nurse takes the letter but stands as if still in doubt. Tatyana motions her to go. The Nurse goes to the door, stands there a moment considering, then comes back again. Finally she signifies that she understands and leaves the room. Tatyana sits down at the table and, resting her elbows on it, again becomes lost in thought. [16, 10]

Scene Three. *Another part of the Larin estate. Thick lilac and acacia bushes, untidy flower beds and an old bench. In the background, peasant girls are gathering berries among the bushes and singing.*

No. 11 Chorus of Girls.

GIRLS

Dear companions, come this way, Join us in the games we play. Choose a happy melody Suited to our revelry. Sing our favourite roundelay For the harvest holiday.	[17] Devitsy, krasavitsy, Dushen'ki, podruzhen'ki! Razygraites', devitsy, Razgulyaites', milye! Zatyanite pesenku Pesenku zavetnuyu,

If a handsome lad comes near,	Zamanite molodtsa,
Let us try to lure him here.	K khorovodu nashemu!
When he's seen us from afar	Kak zamanim molodtsa,
He'll discover where we are.	Kak zavidim izdali —,
If he follows in pursuit,	Razbezhimtes', milye,
Pelt him gaily with your fruit;	Zakidaem vishen'em,
All the berries you can find,	Vishen'em, malinoyu,
Summer fruit of every kind.	Krasnoyu smorodinoi!
As the lad is chased away	Ne khodi podslushivat'
See that he is teased, and say,	Pesenki zavetnye,
'Never come again to spy	Ne khodi podsmatrivat'
On the girlish games we play!'	Igry nashi devich'i!

No. 12 Scene and Aria./Tatyana enters, running quickly, and throws herself, exhausted, on the bench.

TATYANA

Onegin! Here! To see me!	Zdes' on, zdes' Evgenii!
Oh, heavens, what must he think of me?	O bozhe, bozhe, chto podumal on!
What will his answer be?	Chto skazhet on? Akh, dlya chevo,
Why did I write and yield to love so easily?	Stenan'yu vnyav dushi bol'noi,
What foolishness took hold of me	Ne sovladav sama s soboi,
And made me send him such a letter?	Emu pis'mo ya napisala?
It's certain now! My heart foretells it;	Da, serdtse mne teper' skazalo,
The fatal tempter I adore	Chto nasmeyotsya nado mnoi
Will now despise me evermore!	Moi soblaznitel' rokovoi!
O God above, I'm so unhappy,	O, bozhe moi, kak ya neschastna,
I'm so forlorn!	Kak ya zhalka! . . .
He's here, I know it!	Shagi . . . vsyo blizhe . . .
Yes, it is he! It is he!	Da, eto on . . . eto on!

Onegin enters. Tatyana jumps to her feet and Onegin approaches her. She lowers her head. He speaks with dignity, calmly and somewhat coldly.

ONEGIN

You wrote a letter —	Vy mne pisali,
Do not deny it!	Ne otpiraites'.
What I read displayed your innocence and feeling,	Ya prochol dushi doverchivoi priznan'ya,
The wealth of love your heart's concealing,	Lyubvi nevinnoi izliyan'ya,
And I was touched by what you said.	Mne vasha iskrennost' mila;
It stirred within me once again	Ona v volnen'e privela
An old and sensitive emotion.	Davno umolknuvshie chuvstva.
Yet I must ask you to reflect;	No vas khvalit' ya ne khochu;
Surely it can't be thought correct	Ya za neyo vam otplachu
To write so frankly to a stranger.	Priznan'em takzhe bez iskusstva.
So hear what I now have to say,	Primite zh ispoved' moyu:
Then you can judge me as you may.	Sebya na sud vam otdayu.

TATYANA

Oh, heavens! How distressing and how painful!	O bozhe, kak obidno i kak bol'no!

She sinks down on the bench.

ONEGIN

Were I the sort who had intended	[18] Kogda by zhizn' domashnim krugom
To lead a calm domestic life;	Ya ogranichit' zakhotel,
If lasting happiness depended	Kogda b mne byt' otsom, suprugom
On seeking out a perfect wife,	Priyatnyi zhrebii povedel, —
Then doubtless I'd agree	To, verno b, krome vas odnoi
That only you could share my life with me.	Nevesty ne iskal inoi.
But I'm not made for warm affection,	No ya ne sozdan dlya blazhenstva,
And as for wedlock, even less;	Emu chuzhda dusha moya;

And though I value your perfection
I fear I'd cause you much distress.
In fact, and this I've now decided,
To marry you would be misguided.
At first my love would be untold,
But time would make it soon grow cold.
Imagine, then, the thorny roses
Hymen might scatter in our way,
Who knows, perhaps for many a day!
My soul was destined to discover
It sought no other;
That fate decrees for good or ill.
I'll always love you as a brother,
Yes, as a brother,
Or yet maybe more dearly still.
I promise you, maybe more dearly still.
I beg you not to feel rejected;
Your confidence will be respected.
Believe me, all I say is true.
But try to practise self-control;
For some men, unlike me,
Abuse such youthful innocence as yours.

Naprasny vashi sovershenstva,
Ikh nedostoin vovse ya.
Pover'te, sovest' v tom porukoi,
Supruzhestvo nam budet mukoi.
Ya, skol'ko ni lyubil by vas,
Privyknuv, razlyublyu totchas.
Sudite zh vy, kakie rosy
Nam zagotovit Gimenei
I, mozhet byt', na mnogo dnei!
[19] Mechtam i godam net vosvrata,
Akh, net vozvrata,
Ne obnovlyu dushi moei!
Ya vas lyublyu lyubov'yu brata,
Lyubov'yu brata,
Il', mozhet byt', eshcho nezhnei!
Il', mozhet byt', eshcho nezhnei,
Póslushaite zh menya bez gneva,
Smenit ne raz mladaya deva
Mechtami lyogkie mechty!
Uchites', vlastvovat' soboi;
Ne vsyakii vas, kak ya, poimyot,
Ke bede neopytnost' vedyot!

GIRLS
(in the distance)

Dear companions, come this way,
Join us in the games we play.
Choose a happy melody
Suited to our revelry.
If a handsome lad comes near,
Let us try to lure him here.
If he follows in pursuit,
Pelt him gaily with your fruit;
See that he is teased, and say,
'Never come again to spy
On the girlish games we play!'

[17] Devitsy, krasavitsy,
Dushen'ki, podruzhen'ki!
Razygraites', devitsy,
Razgulyaites', milye.
Kak zamanim molodtsa,
Kak zavidim izdali.
Razbezhimtes', milye,
Zakidaem vishen'em!
Ne khodi podsluchivat',
Ne khodi podsmatrivat'
Igry nashi devich'i!

As the song gradually becomes more distant, Onegin offers his arm to Tatyana; she gives him a long, imploring look, then rises mechanically and goes out meekly, leaning on his arm.

Act Two

Scene One. *A brightly illuminated ballroom in Madame Larina's house. In the centre a chandelier; on the walls, sconces with lighted tallow candles. Guests, in very old-fashioned evening dress, and among them officers, dressed in the military uniform of the 1820s, are dancing a waltz. The older men sit in groups and watch the dancing admiringly. The older women, who are carrying reticules, occupy chairs placed along the walls. Onegin is dancing with Tatyana and Lensky with Olga. Madame Larina moves about continually with the air of a solicitous hostess.*

No. 13 Entr'acte, Waltz and Chorus. [14, 20]

GUESTS

This is superb!	Vot tak syurpriz!
We never had expected	Nikak ne ozhidali
Such splendid company	Voennoi muzyki!
And dancing to a band!	Vesel'e khot' kuda!
We seldom see parties	Davno uzh nas
Such as this one.	Tak ne ugoshchali!
What glorious food/wine,	Na slavu pir,
So tasteful, so well-planned!	Ne pravdal', gospoda?
Yes, it's splendid! Yes, it's splendid!	Bravo, bravo, bravo, bravo!
Simply delightful!	Vot tak syurpriz nam!
What a party, what a party!	Bravo, bravo, bravo, bravo!
We have never been more surprised!	Slavnyi syurpriz dlya nas!

ELDERLY GENTLEMEN

Here in the country we live in seclusion;	V nashikh pomest'yakh ne chasto vstrechaem
Festive occasions and dancing are rare.	Bala vesyolovo radostnyi blesk.
Hunting is usually our only diversion;	Tol'ko okhotoi sebya rasvlekaem:
Makes a nice change from the hounds and the hare!	Lyub nam okhotnichii gomon i tresk.

ELDERLY LADIES

That's all our men-folk consider amusing,	Nu, uzh vesel'e: den' tselyi letayut
Just shooting and fishing and up with the sun;	Po debryam, polyanam, bolotam, kustam!
And then in the evening they're always exhausted,	Ustanut, zalyagut i vsyo otdykhayut,
Yet we who've been working could do with some fun!	I vot razvlechen'e dlya bednykh vsekh dam!

A group of young girls surrounds the Captain.

YOUNG GIRLS

Oh, Trifon Petrovich,	Akh, Trifon Petrovich,
We beg you to tell us	Kak mily vy, pravo!
ʾhe name of your regiment!	My tak blagodarny vam . . .

CAPTAIN

ʾy! But why aren't you dancing?	Polnote-s! Ya sam ochen' schastliv!

YOUNG GIRLS

ʾas asked us to.	Poplyashem na slavu my!

CAPTAIN

ʾies, the pleasure is	Ya tozhe nameren, nachnyomte zh plyasat'!

ʾ Tatyana. The others stop dancing and everyone watches them.

ELDERLY LADIES

ʾ be	Glyan'te-ka, glyan'te-ka! Tantsuyut pizhony!

74

She must find a husband. That's him, for sure!
How sad for Tatyana, for once they are married,
She'll find he's a tyrant. He gambles, what's more!

Davno uzh pora by! Nu, zhenishok!
Kak zhalko Tanyushu! Voz'myot eyo v zheny . . .
I budet tiranit': On, slyshno, igrok!

Onegin quietly passes by them, trying to overhear their conversation.

He's most discourteous and conceited;
The things he says can't be repeated!
He's a freemason, so they say,
And ends up drunk on wine each day.

On — neuch strashnyi, sumasbrodit,
On damam k ruchke ne podkhodit,
On — farmazon, on p'yot odno
Stakanom krasnoe vino!

ONEGIN

So that's your verdict! No more of this!

I vot vam mnen'e! Naslushalsya dovol'no

I'm tired of hearing their dreary gossip.
Serves me right, though, for coming.
Whatever brought me here to this confounded ball?
Yes, what! I can't forgive Vladimir for persuading me
To come, so I'll dance again with Olga,
For that will make him jealous.

Ya raznykh spleten merzkikh!
Po delam mne vsyo eto!
Zachem priekhal ya na etot glupyi bal?

Zachem? Ya ne proshchu Vladimiru uslugu etu!
Budu ukhazhivat' za Ol'goi,
Vzbeshu evo poryadkom!

At this moment, Olga passes by, followed by Lensky.

Here she is.

Vot ona!

(to Olga)

Allow me!

Proshu vas!

LENSKY
(to Olga)

But you had promised *me* this dance!

Vy obeshchali mne teper'!

ONEGIN
(to Lensky)

You're mistaken there, my friend!

Oshibsya, verno, ty!

He dances with Olga.

LENSKY

She's smiling at him!
I must be dreaming! Olga!
What's come over you?

Akh, chto takoe!
Glazam ne veryu! Ol'ga!
Bozhe, chto so mnoi!

GUESTS

Such a party,
Such a surprise!
What delightful dancing!
The party's at its height.
This is superb!
We never had expected
Such splendid company
And dancing to a band!

Vot tak syurpriz!
Nikak ne ozhidali
Voennoi muzyki!
Vesel'e khot' kuda!
Davno uzh nas
Tak ne ugoshchali!
Na slavu pir,
Ne pravdal', gospoda?

Not for years have we seen such a party;
This is truly perfection, beyond all expectation!
Hail to music, hail to song!
We'll feast and dance the whole night long!

Bravo, bravo, bravo, bravo!
Vot tak syurpriz nam! Bravo!

Bravo, bravo, bravo, bravo!
Slavnyi syurpriz dlya nas!

No. 14 Scene and Triquet's Couplets. / Lensky goes up to Olga, who has just finished dancing with Onegin.

LENSKY

How can I have deserved to be so taunted by you?

Uzhel', ya zasluzhil ot vas nasmeshku etu?

75

Oh, Olga, why do you torture me like this?	Akh, Ol'ga, kak zhestoki vy so mnoi!
What have I done?	Chto sdelal ya?

OLGA

I can't imagine what you're referring to!	Ne ponimayu, v chom vinovata ya?

LENSKY

Throughout the evening your waltzes,	Vse ekosezy, vse val'sy
Yes, all of them, were with Onegin!	S Oneginym vy tantsovali!
And yet when I asked, you just ignored me.	Ya priglashal vas, no byl otvergnut!

OLGA

Vladimir, this is foolish;	Vladimir, eto stranno:
Don't let a dance upset you so.	Iz pustyakov ty serdish'sya!

LENSKY

What! Don't you think I care?	Kak! Iz-za pustyakov?
Am I supposed to watch quite indifferently	Uzheli ravnodushno ya videt' mog,
While you make eyes at him and flirt like some coquette!	Kogda smeyalas' ty, koketnichaya s nim?
He held you far too closely	K tebe on naklonyalsya,
And pressed your hand in his.	I ruku zhal tebe! . . .
I saw it all!	Ya videl vsyo!

OLGA

Oh, this is stupid jealousy and pure imagination!	Vsyo eto pustyaki i bred! Revnuesh' ty naprasno:
I only talked to him;	My tak boltali s nim.
He has such charm.	On ochen' mil!

LENSKY

So, it's charm!	Dazhe mil!
Ah, Olga, you no longer love me.	Akh, Ol'ga, ty menya ne lyubish'!

OLGA

Don't be so silly!	Kakoi ty strannyi!

LENSKY

No, you do not love me.	Ty menya ne lyubish' . . .

Onegin approaches them.

Will you dance the *cotillon* with me?	Kotil'on so mnoi tantsuesh' ty?

ONEGIN

No, with me!	Net, so mnoi!
For I shall hold you to your promise.	Ne pravda l', slovo vy mne dali?

OLGA

And I mean to keep it.	I sderzhu ya slovo!

(to Lensky)

Let this be your lesson for being so jealous!	Vot vam nakazan'e za revnost' vashu!

LENSKY

Olga!	Ol'ga!

OLGA

It's no use!	Ni za chto!

Monsieur Triquet is seen in the background, surrounded by a group of girls.

Just look how all the girls	Glyadite-ka:
Are gathering round Monsieur Triquet.	Vse baryshni idut syuda s Trike!

	ONEGIN
Who's he?	Kto on!
	OLGA
A Frenchman who lives here in the village.	Frantsuz, zhivyot u Kharlikova!
	GIRLS
Monsieur Triquet! Monsieur Triquet!	Monsieur Triquet, Monsieur Triquet!
Chantez de grâce un couplet!	*Chantez de grâce un couplet!*
	TRIQUET
By chance I 'ave with me a song.	Kuplet imeet ya s soboi.
But first, where is la Mademoiselle?	No gde, skazhite, Mademoiselle?
Without she 'ere I cannot start,	On dolzhen byt' peredo mnoi,
Car le couplet est fait pour elle!	*Car le couplet est fait pour elle!*
	GIRLS
Here she is! Here she is!	Vot ona! Vot ona!
	TRIQUET
Aha, *voilà* ze lovely birthday queen!	Aha! Voilà tsaritsa etot den'!
Mesdames, I'm ready to *commence*;	Mesdames! Ya budu nachinait'!
Remarquez bien my French nuance!	Proshu teper' mne ne meshait!

All the guests form a circle and Tatyana is placed in the middle. Triquet addresses the following* couplets to her; she is embarrassed and wants to escape but is prevented from doing so. He sings with great expression.

[21]

'A cette fête conviée,	Kakoi prekrasnyi etot den',
De celle dont le jour est fêté	Kogda v sei derevenskii sen'
Contemplons le charme et la beauté.	Prosypalsya belle Tatiana!
Son aspect doux et enchanteur	I mi priekhali, syuda —
Répand sur nous tous sa lueur;	Devits, i dam, i gospoda —
De la voir quel plaisir, quel bonheur!	Posmotret', kak rastsvetait ona!
Brillez, brillez toujours, belle Tatiana!'	Vi — rosa, vi — rosa, vi — rosa, belle Tatiana!

	GUESTS
Bravo, bravo, bravo, Monsieur Triquet!	Bravo, bravo, bravo, Monsieur Triquet!
Your singing is delightful;	Kuplet vash prevoskhoden
A fitting tribute for the day!	I ochen', ochen' milo spet!

---

* These verses in broken Russian and French are literally translated in this footnote. The pure French verses are not translations but alternative texts approved by the composer. It is unclear which Tchaikovsky preferred (see p. 26).

How beautiful this day,
When into this village canopy ['village' possibly an intentional error for 'wooded']
Awakened belle Tatiana! [verb is misspelled and in wrong gender; meaning is as
      odd as it sounds in English]
And we came here, ['we' misspelled]
Girls and ladies and gentlemen,
To look at how she is blossoming. ['blossoming' misspelled]
You are a rose, you are a rose, belle Tatiana! ['you' misspelled]

We wish much to be happy,
To be forever the fairy de ces rives,
Never to be bored, sick!
And let her, among her bonheurs
Not forget her serviteur [verb misspelled]
And all her girlfriends!
You are a rose, you are a rose, belle Tatiana!

'Que le sort comble ses désirs, | Zhelaem mnogo byt' schastliv.
Que la joie, les jeux, les plaisirs | Byt' vechno feya de ces rives,
Fixent sur ses lèvres le sourire! | Nikogda ne byt' skuchna, bol'na!
Que sur le ciel de ce pays, | I pust', sredi svoikh bonheurs
Étoile qui toujours brille et luit, | Ne zabyvait svoi serviteur
Elle éclaire nos jours et nos nuits! | I vse svoi podrug ona!
Brillez, brillez toujours, belle Tatiana!' | Vi — rosa, vi — rosa, vi — rosa, belle
| Tatiana!

Bravo, bravo, bravo, Monsieur Triquet! | Bravo, bravo, bravo, Monsieur Triquet!
Your singing is delightful; | Kuplet vash prevoskhoden
A fitting tribute for the day! | I ochen', ochen' milo spet!

Monsieur Triquet bows his acknowledgements and then, on his knees, offers the song to the embarrassed Tatyana.

No. 15 Mazurka and Scene.

Messieurs! Mesdames! | Messieurs, mesdames,
I beg you to take your partners, | Mesta zanyat' izvol'te,
For now we have the *cotillon.* | Seichas nachnyotsya kotil'on!
| (*to Tatyana*)
Allow me, pray! | Pozhaluite!

[22]

They lead off the dance. The guests pair off and dance. Onegin and Olga sit down towards the front of the stage. Lensky stands, lost in thought behind them. After dancing a turn with Olga, Onegin conducts her to her seat and then turns to Lensky as if he had only just noticed him.

Why aren't you dancing, Lensky? | Ty ne tantsuesh' Lensky?
Even Hamlet was not as gloomy! | Chail'd Garol'dom stoish' kakim-to!
What's wrong with you? | Chto s toboi?

Why, nothing! Can't you see? | So mnoi? Nichevo!
I'm trying to admire | Lyubyus' ya toboi,
The way you show your friendship! | Kakoi ty drug prekrasnyi!

Is that so? | Kakovo?
I had expected quite a different answer. | Ne ozhidal prisnan'ya ya takovo!
Why are you sulking, then? | Za chto ty duesh'sya?

Lensky at first answers quietly, but gradually his tone becomes more and more embittered and angry.

What nonsense! I'm not sulking. | Ya duyus'? O, nimalo!
I've watched with fascination how you lure | Lyubyus', ya, kak slov svoikh igroi
These unsuspecting girls with flattering compliments | I svetskoi boltovnei ty kruzhish' golovy
And, trifling with their feelings, humiliate them. | I devochek smushchaesh' pokoi dushevnyi.

The guests gradually stop dancing as they become aware of the conversation between Onegin and Lensky.

First you break the heart of poor Tatyana; | Vidno, dlya tebya odnoi Tat'yany malo!
Then you pick on Olga | Iz lyubvi ko mne
And amuse yourself by compromising her. | Ty, verno, khochesh' Ol'gu pogubit',
You'll quickly turn her head | Smutit' eyo pokoi, a tam

78

And make your conquest, then laugh at her.
What a man of honour!

Smeyat'sya nad neyu zhe! . . .
Akh, kak chestno eto!

ONEGIN
(with a sneer, but calmly)

Come, you've lost your senses, Lensky!

Chto? Da ty s uma soshol!

LENSKY

Oh, thank you! I'm first of all insulted
And then openly declared a lunatic!

Prekrasno! Menya zh ty oskorblyaesh' —
I menya zhe ty zovyosh' pomeshannym!

Everybody stops dancing.

GUESTS

What's he saying? What's the matter?

Chto takoe? V chom tam delo?

The guests leave their places and surround the quarrelling men.

LENSKY

Onegin, you are no more my friend!
I hereby sever all ties of friendship with you,
For you are beneath contempt!

Onegin! Vy bol'she mne ne drug!
Byt' blizoim s vami ya ne zhelayu bol'she!
Ya . . . ya presirayu vas!

GUESTS

How did this quarrel come about,
What's more, at such a splendid party?
Let us hope it won't turn into something serious!

Vot neozhidannyi syurpriz!
Kakaya ssora zakipela:
U nikh poshlo ne v shutku delo!

ONEGIN
(drawing Lensky slightly to one side)

Now, Lensky, listen; you're distraught!
Don't let us cause all this fuss and quarrel over nothing.
I never wanted to embarrass you
And must protest, had no such base intention.
You are my friend.

Poslushai, Lensky, ty ne prav, ty ne prav!
Dovol'no nam privlekat' vniman'e nashei ssoroi!
Ya ne smutil eshcho nichei pokoi
I, priznayus', zhelan'ya ne imeyu
Evo smushchat'.

LENSKY
(with increasing passion)

If that is so, why did you press her hand,
And whisper something?
She blushed as she answered you.
What was it you suggested?

Togda zachem zhe ty ei ruku zhal,
Sheptal ei chto-to?
Krasnela, smeyas', ona . . .
Chto, chto ty govoril ei?

ONEGIN

Enough, now! Don't be foolish;
The guests are listening.

Poslushai, eto glupo!
Nas okruzhayut!

LENSKY
(beside himself)

What is that to me? You publicly insult me,
So I insist on satisfaction!

Chto za delo mne! Ya vami oskorblyon
I satisfaktsii ya trebuyu!

GUESTS

What is it? What's the matter?
Who can tell us what has happened?

V chom delo? Rasskazhite,
Rasskazhite, chto sluchilos'.

LENSKY

I can!
So hear me now.
I simply asked Onegin

Prosto . . .
Ya trebuyu,
Chtob gospodin Onegin

What was the reason for his conduct, And he refused to answer me. I therefore say to him, accept my challenge!	Mne obyasnil svoi postupki! On ne zhelaet. etovo I ya proshu evo prinyat' moi vyzov!

Madame Larina pushes her way through the crowd and addresses Lensky.

MADAME LARINA

A challenge! Oh, have pity! Do not quarrel here in my house!	O bozhe! V nashem dome! Poshchadite, poshchadite!

No. 16 Finale.

LENSKY

Here in your house! Here in your house!	[6] V vashem dome!... V vashem dome!

(with great feeling)

It was here in these peaceful surroundings That my leisure was spent as a child; It was here that I first learnt the meaning Of a love that was tender and mild. But this evening I've lost my illusions And discovered that life's not a dream, And that honour is just a delusion.	V vashem dome, kak sny zolotye Moi detskii gody tekli; V vashem dome vkusil ya vpervye Radost' chistoi i svetloi lyubvi. No sevodnya uznal ya drugoe: Ya izvedal, chto zhizn' — ne roman, Chest' — lish' zvuk, druzhba — slovo pustoe,
Even friendship that seemed so fraternal Can be shattered and grossly betrayed!	Oskorbitel'nyi, zhalkii obman! Oskorbitel'nyi, zhalkii obman!

ONEGIN

Deep in my heart I must concede That I have acted foolishly. What made me do so? Sadly now I can realise that for Lensky Love is something poetic, And that passions, when they are sincere, must not be trifled with. By taunting him in front of Olga I've earned the hatred of my friend.	Naedinie s svoei dushoi Ya nedovolen sam soboi! Nad etoi strast'yu robkoi, nezhnoi Ya slishkom poshutil nebrezhno! Vsem serdtsem yunoshu lyubya, Ya b dolzhen, ya b dolzhen pokazat' sebya Ne myachikom predrassuzhdenii, No muzhem s chest'yu i umom!

TATYANA

What I have seen has made me wretched, And I'm oppressed with jealous anguish; For such behaviour I cannot understand. Jealous anguish gives way to despair, My anguish gives way to despair, As if an icy hand had gripped my heart in torment!	Potryasena ya, um ne mozhet Ponyat' Evgeniya... Trevozhit Menya trevozhit revnivaya toska... Akh, terzaet mne serdtse toska! Kak kholodnaya ch'ya-to ruka, Ona mne szhala serdtse bol'no tak, zhestoko!

OLGA & MADAME LARINA

The evening may well end in horror If they should really fight a duel!	Boyus' chtoby vosled vesel'yu Ne zavershilas' noch' duel'yu!

GUESTS

Poor young Lensky! What a tragedy!	Bednyi Lensky! Bednyi yunosha!

ONEGIN

I'm punished for my thoughtless conduct!	Ya slishkom poshutil nebrezho!

LENSKY

Once I loved what I thought was perfection, Like an angel, as fair as the day.	Ya uznal zdes', chto deva krasoyu Mozhet byt', tochno angel, mila

Now I know it was purely deception,
For by nature she's a devil who'll cheat
and betray!

I prekrasna, kak den', no dushoyu ...
No dushoyu ... tochno demon, kovarna
i zla!

TATYANA

All is over now, no further hope is left!
Yet death because of him is welcome,
And sweeter than living without him!
Yes, death is now certain, my heart has
foretold it.
I shall die, and yet I don't complain.
Hereafter no foolish illusions remain.
I realise that nothing can bring us
together,
And death is now certain to part us for
ever!

Akh, pogibla ya, mne serdtse govorit
No gibel' ot nevo lyubezna!
Pogibnu, pogibnu, — mne serdtze
skazalo!
Roptat' ya ne smeyu, ne smeyu!
Akh, zachem roptat', zachem roptat'!
Ne mozhet, ne mozhet on schast'ya mne
dat'!
Pogibnu, pogibnu, mne serdtse skazalo,
Mne serdtse skazalo, roptat' ya ne
smeyu, ne smeyu!

OLGA

Why must all men behave the same
And think of duels as a game?
They're far too quick to pick a quarrel.
Why do Onegin and Lensky act like
fools
And think that honour's made of rules?
Vladimir's jealousy will choke him,
Yet I've done nothing to provoke him,
not I.
How like a man to fly into a passion.
They're foolish, impulsive, they argue and
quarrel,
But never a moment consider what
fighting may lead to.

Akh, krov' v muzhchinakh goryacha, —
Oni reshayut vsyo splecha,
Bez ssor ne mogut ostavat'sya!
Akh, krov' v muzhchinakh goryacha, —
Oni reshayut vsyo splesha!
Dusha v nyom revnost'yu obyata,
No ya ni v chom ne vinovata, ni v chom!
Akh! Ya ni v chom ne vinovata!
Muzhchiny ne mogut' bez ssory ostat'sya
Povzdoryat, posporyat, — seichas zhe
i drat'sya gotovy!

MADAME LARINA

Why must all men behave the same
And think of duels as a game?
They're far too quick to pick a quarrel.
Why do Onegin and Lensky act like
fools
And think that honour's made of rules?
The evening may well end in horror,
If they should really fight a duel.
Oh, the shame of it is cruel!
Why are the young always the same?
So foolish, impulsive, they argue and
quarrel,
But never a moment consider what
fighting may lead to.

Akh, krov' v muzhchinakh goryacha, —
Oni reshayut vsyo splecha,
Bez ssor ne mogut ostavat'sya!
Akh, molodyozh' kak goryacha,
Oni reshayut vsyo splecha!
Boyus' chto by vo sled vesel' yu,
Ne zavershilas' noch' duel'yu,
Molodyozh' tak goryacha!
Akh! molodyozh, tak goryacha!
Bez ssory ne mogut ni chasu ostat'sya!
Povzdoryat, posporyat, seichas zhe
i drat'sya gotovy!

GUESTS

Oh, what a shame! It's really cruel
To spoil our party with their duel!
Young men today are all the same;
They've only got themselves to blame!
Yes, only got themselves to blame.
Why are the young always the same?
So foolish, impulsive; they argue and
quarrel,
But never a moment consider what
fighting may lead to.

Uzhel' teper' vosled vesel'yu
Ikh ssora konchitsya duel'yu?
No molodyozh' tak goryacha, —
Oni reshayut vsyo splecha,
Oni reshayut vsyo splecha!
Akh! molodyozh', tak goryacha!
Bez ssory ne mogut ni chasu ostat'sya,
Povzdoryat, posporyat, — seichas zhe
i dratsya gotovy!

ONEGIN

Deep in my heart I must concede
That I have acted foolishly.

Naedine s svoei dushoi
Ya nedovolen sam soboi!

What made me do so? Now I realise That Lensky's love was too poetic; That passions, when they are sincere, Are never to be trifled with. By taunting him in front of Olga I've merely succeeded in rousing The anger and hatred of one I loved. Now it's too late to make amends; I'm honour bound to answer for my actions.	Nad etoi strast'yu robkoi, nezhoi, Ya slishkom poshutil nebrezhno! Vsem serdtsem yunoshu lyubya, Ya b dolzhen pokazat' sebya Ne myachikom predrassuzhdenii, Ne pilkim, ne pilkim rebyonkom, No muzhem vzh zrel'im ya vinovat! No delat' nechevo, teper' Ya dolzhen otvechat' na oskorblen'ya!

LENSKY

Ah, Olga, you never were to blame, So forgive me, my angel, my darling! The fault was Onegin's for acting so basely, And he shall be punished!	Akh, net, ty nevinna, angel moi! Ty nevinna, nevinna, moi angel! On nizkii, kovarnyi, bezdushnyi predatel', — On budet nakazan!

*

ONEGIN
(to Lensky)

Your challenge I accept. So be it.
Everything you've said is ludicrous, yes,
  ludicrous,
And you deserve a lesson for such folly!
	K uslugam vashim ya! Dovol'no, —
	Vyslushal ya vas: bezumny vy, bezumny
	  vy,
	I vam urok posluzhit k ispravlen'yu!

LENSKY

We'll see tomorrow exactly Who deserved the lesson! Perhaps I am a fool . . . but you . . . You . . . lack honour, you seducer!	Itak, do zavtra! Posmotrim, kto kovo prouchit! Puskai bezumets ya . . . no vy . . . Vy . . . bezchestnyi soblaznitel'!

ONEGIN

Hold your tongue, sir, or I shall kill you!	Zamolchite . . . il' ya ub'yu vas! . . .

Madame Larina, Olga and some of the guests hold Lensky back. Tatyana is in tears. Onegin throws himself at Lensky; they are separated. Onegin goes to one side and turns his back on Lensky.

GUESTS

What a disgrace! Fighting a duel!
It must be prevented; we shall not allow
  it!
Until they are calmer we'll stop them from
  leaving!
Otherwise there'll surely be a scandal!
	Chto za skandal! My ne dopustim
	Dueli mezh nimi, krovavoi raspravy;
	
	Ikh prosto otsyuda ne pustim. Derzhite,
	
	Da, ikh prosto iz domu ne pustim.

OLGA

Vladimir, stop your quarrel, I implore you!	Vladimir, uspokoisya, umolyayu!

LENSKY

Ah, Olga, Olga, farewell for ever!	Akh, Ol'ga, Ol'ga! Proshchai navek!

GUESTS

Now for bloodshed!	Byt' dueli!

Lensky rushes out. Onegin also leaves quickly. Olga runs after Lensky but falls fainting. Everyone rushes to help her.

---

* Extra stanzas in the same vein for this ensemble were written and set to music by Tchaikovsky in his manuscript full score. The passage was never published in his lifetime, however, and did not appear in print until the 1946 piano score in the Complete Collected Works.

Scene Two. *A rustic watermill on the banks of a wooded stream. Early morning; the sun has barely risen. It is winter. When the curtain rises Lensky and Zaretsky are already on stage. Lensky sits under a tree, lost in thought. Zaretsky walks up and down impatiently.*

No. 17 Introduction, Scene and Aria. [23, 25]

ZARETSKY

What's happened? Where can your opponent be? Is he coming?

Nu, chto zhe? Kazhetsya, protivnik vash ne yavilsya?

LENSKY

Clearly he's delayed.

Yavitsya seichas.

[25]

ZARETSKY

Well, nonetheless, I find it most discourteous!
He should be here, it's after six.
I wonder if he's lost his way?

No vsyo zhe eto stranno mne nemnozhko,

Chto net evo: sed'moi ved' chas!
Ya dumal chto on zhdyot uzh nas!

Zaretsky walks over to the mill and enters into conversation with the miller, who has just appeared in the background. The miller shows him the wheel, millstones etc.. Lensky continues to sit and meditate. [6]

LENSKY

How far, how far away you seem now,
O happy days when I was young!

Kuda, kuda, kuda vy udalilis',
Vesny moei zlatyi dni?

He rises and comes forward.

Shall I survive the day that's dawning? [25]
I vainly try to read its warning.
It shrouds itself in mystery!
No matter, this is fate's decree.
My rival's shot may well dispatch me
Or miss its mark and pass me by.
So be it; death will come to claim me
At the moment of her choosing.
Welcome the day when sorrow calls;
Welcome the night when silence falls.
Tomorrow's sky will stretch unclouded;
Mankind will start another day.
But I, by that time, may be shrouded
And lie interred within my grave.
As sluggish Lethe bears me downward
My name will cease to be remembered,
And fade from memory . . . save yours,
   Olga!

Chto den' gryadushchii mne gotovit?
Evo moi vzor naprasno lovit,
V glubokoi t'me taitsya on.
Net nuzhdy; prav sud'by zakon!
Padu li ya, streloi pronzyonnyi,
Il' mimo proletit ona, —
Vsyo blago: bdeniya i sna
Prikhodit chas opredelyonnyi!
Blagosloven i den' zabot,
Blagosloven i t'my prikhod!
Blesnet zautra luch dennitsy
I zaigraet yapkii den';
A ya, byt' mozhet, ya grobnitsy
Soidu v tainstvennuyu sen',
I pamyat' yunovo poeta
Poglotit medlennaya Leta,
Zabudet mir menya, no ty . . . Ty!*

(with great feeling)

Will you then come, my angel, my beloved,
To shed a tear where I am lying
And say there: 'Once we were in love,
But now he watches from above
As I lament his early dying'?
Ah, Olga, once we were in love!
To you alone I have devoted
A poet's feelings and emotion.
Ah, Olga, once we were in love!
Beloved friend, my promised bride,
I wait for you! Your bridegroom waits
To greet his chosen bride. Oh, come!
Oh, come to me, my chosen bride!
Oh, come, oh, come, be at my side!
How far, how far away you seem now,
O happy days when I was young!

Skazhi, pridesh' li, deva krasoty,

Slezu prolit' nad rannei urnoi
I dumat': on menya lyubil!
On mne edinoi posvyatil
Rassvet pechal'nyi zhizni burnoi!
Akh, Ol'ga, ya tebya lyubil! . . .
Tebe edinoi posvyatil
Rassvet pechal'nyi zhizni burnoi!
Akh, Ol'ga, ya tebya lyubil! . . .
Serdechnyi drug, zhelannyi drug,
Pridi! Pridi! Zhelannyi drug,
Pridi! Ya tvoi suprug! Pridi!
Ya zhdu tebya, zhelannyi drug,
Pridi! Pridi! Ya tvoi suprug!
Kuda, kuda vy udalilis',
Zlatye dni moei vesny!

---

* This line is sometimes varied to 'Ty, Ol'ga!' but see Challis p. 42.

83

No. 18 Duel Scene. / *Zaretsky comes forward and speaks to Lensky.*

ZARETSKY

Ah, here they are!   A, vot oni!
But who's your friend brought with him?   No s kem zhe vash priyatel'?
I can't make him out.   Ne razberu!

Onegin enters with his servant Guillot, who carries the pistols. Onegin bows to the other two.

ONEGIN

I trust you'll both excuse me;   Proshu vas isvinenya!
Clearly I've kept you waiting.   Ya opozdal nemnosgko.

ZARETSKY

No matter! Where, sir, is your second?   Pozvol'te! Gde zh vash sekundant?
In my view duels are an art   V duelyakh klassik ya, pedant;
And must, as such, be fought correctly.   Lyublyu metodu ya iz chuvstva,
Therefore I see to it that no one meets his I cheloveka rastyanut' pozvolyu ya
  end
Just anyhow, but by the code, and   Ne kak-nibud', no v strogikh pravilakh
  circumspectly.   iskusstva.
Established custom is the best.   Po vsem predan'yam stariny!

ONEGIN

Sir, I am suitably impressed.   Chto pokhvalit' my v vas dolzhny!
Where is my second?   Moi sekundant?
Here he is — Monsieur Guillot.   Vot on — Monsieur Guillot!
As you can see, he's just my servant;   Ya mne predvizhnu vosrazhenii
But you've no reason to object: Na predstavlenie moyo:
He doesn't know the *code duello*   Khot' chelovek on neizvestnyi
But he's a worthy, honest fellow.   No uzh, konechno, malyi chestnyi.

Guillot bows deeply; Zaretsky returns his bow coldly.

Well, shall we start?   Chto zh, nachinat'?

LENSKY

Why, yes, by all means.   Nachnyom, pozhalui.

Zaretsky and Guillot step aside to discuss the conditions of the duel. Lensky and Onegin stand waiting, not looking at each other. [25]

LENSKY & ONEGIN

We fight to satisfy our honour   [26] Vragi! . . . Davno li drug ot druga
And thirst to shed each other's blood.   Nas zhazhda krovi otvela?
Yet formerly we shared as brother   Davno li my chasy dosuga,
With brother in everything we could,   Trapezu, i mysli, i dela
For such is friendship. Now, in anger,   Delili druzhno? Nyne zlobno,
Like deadly rivals bent on vengeance,   Vragam nasledstvennym podobno,
Each of us silently prepares   My drug dlya druga v tishine
To kill his adversary if need be.   Gotovym gibel' khladnokrovno . . .
Ah!   Akh!
Why can't we stop our anger's flood   Ne zasmeyat'sya l' nam, poka
Before our hands are stained with blood,   Ne obagrilasya ruka
And leave together reunited!   Ne rasoitis' li polyubovno?
No! No! No! No!   Net! Net! Net! Net!

Zaretsky and Guillot have loaded the pistols and measured the distance. Zaretsky separates the adversaries and hands them the pistols. Everything is done in silence. Guillot, in embarrassment, hides behind a tree. [6]

ZARETSKY

And now, draw closer!   Teper' skhodites'!

[25]

He claps his hands three times. The adversaries, who have not yet taken aim, take four steps forward. Onegin, as he advances, raises his pistol. As he does so, Lensky begins to take aim. Onegin fires; Lensky staggers, falls and drops his pistol. Zaretsky runs to him and examines him intently. Onegin also rushes towards his dying adversary.

ONEGIN
(in a stifled voice)

Not dead? Ubit?

ZARETSKY

Yes, dead. Ubit!

Aghast, Onegin clasps his head in his hands. [25]

Onegin (Wolfgang Brendel) stares at the dead body of Lensky (Claes-Haaken Ahnsjö), Munich, 1977 (photo: Sabine Toepffer)

Act Three

Scene One. *One of the side-rooms in the house of a rich nobleman in St Petersburg.*

No. 19 Polonaise. [27] / *Guests dance a polonaise; at the end they sit down. Others form groups and converse.*

No. 20 Scene and Aria. / *Onegin stands by a wall on the right, downstage.*

ONEGIN

Here, too, I'm bored!	I zdes' mne skuchno. Blesk i sueta
Bored by all this worldly ostentation.	Bol'shovo sveta ne rasseyut vechnoi.
Nothing can extinguish the anguish of my soul!	Tomitel'noi toski!

He comes further downstage.

I've killed the only friend I valued	Ubiv na poedinke druga,
And, though I've property and wealth,	Dozhiv bez tseli, bez trudov
I'm growing weary with myself.	Do dvadtsati shesti godov,
I'm tired of indolence and leisure;	Tomyas' bezdeistviem dosuga,
I've drifted without aim in life	Bez sluzhby, bez zheny, bez del,
And have no family or wife.	Sebya zanyat' ya ne sumel.
Boredom began to make me restless;	Mnoi ovladelo bespokoistvo,
Each day brought discontent and spleen,	Okhota k peremene mest,
Until the languor of my spirits	Ves'ma muchitel'noe svoistvo,
Impelled me to a change of scene.	Nemnogikh dobrovol'nyi krest!
I left behind, in disillusion,	Ostavil ya svoi selen'ya,
The countryside, with its seclusion,	Lesov i niv uedinen'e,
Where I now saw at every bend	Gde okravavlennaya ten'
The spectre of my murdered friend!	Ko mne yavlyalas' kazhdyi den'!
And so I set out on my travels	Ya nachal stranstvovat' bez seli,
And started wandering without aim.	Dostupnyi chuvstvu odnomu . . .
But soon I realised, in despair,	I chto zh? K neschast'yu moemu,
That travel too was just as boring!	I stranstviya mne nadoeli!
So I returned here, paid a call,	Ya vozvratilsya i popal,
And joined them at this tedious ball!	Kak Chatsky, s korablya na bal!

GUESTS*

[Who is that man amid this splendour,	[Skazhite, kto v tolpe izbrannoi
Who stands so silent and dejected?	Stoit bezmolvnyi i tumannyi?
Who can it be? Is it Onegin?	Kto on takov? Uzhel' Onegin?
No question!	Da, tochno!
But why's he here? Will he be different,	Vsyo tot zhe l' on? Il' usmirilsya,
Or still maintain his pose and play the madcap?	Il' korchit takzhe chudaka?
Remembering his former insolent behaviour,	Skazhite, chem on vozvratilsya,
What is the role he's now assuming?	Chem nam on predstabitsya, poka?
A cosmopolitan? Melmoth? A patriot?	Mel'motom? Kosmopolitom? Patriotom?
Man of action? Childe Harold?	Garol'dom il' khanzhoi?
Or does he wear a different mask —	Il' maskoi shchegol'nyot inoi?
That of a normal, decent fellow?	Il' prosto budet dobryi malyi?
No matter! No matter!]	Smotrite, smotrite!]

The guests dance an Ecossaise. As they finish, Prince Gremin enters with Tatyana on his arm.

GUESTS

The Princess Gremina! Make way there!	Knyaginya Gremina! Smotrite!

---

* In the first edition of the opera Onegin's monologue is followed by this short choral link into the entrance of Tatyana. Responding to a request from the Maryinsky Theatre for an extra dance, Tchaikovsky replaced this in 1885 with the Ecossaise, which is played both here and at the end of the scene (instead of the turbulent exit music for Onegin). As this original version is occasionally preferred, it is given here in brackets.

Tatyana sits on a sofa. Guests of both sexes come up to her continually and greet her with deference.

SOME MEN

Which is she, though? | [28] Kotoraya?

LADIES

Why, there she is! | Syuda, vzglyanite!

MEN

The one who's standing by the Prince. | Vot ta, chto sela u stola!
What simple elegance she has! | Bespechnoi prelest'yu mila!

ONEGIN
(looking intently at Tatyana)

Is that Tatyana? Surely . . . no! | Uzhel' Tatyana? Tochno! . . . Net!
What? From that dull provincial village? | Kak! Iz glushi stepnykh selenii?
It cannot be! How unaffected, | Ne mozhet byt' . . . I kak prosta,
And how composed, and how noble! | Kak velichava, kak nebrezhna!
Her dignity would grace a queen! | Tsaritsei kazhetsya ona!

Tatyana turns to those near her, indicating with a look that she is referring to Onegin, whom Prince Gremin has just approached.

TATYANA

Who is that gentleman, the dark one | Skazhite, kto eto? Tam . . . s muzhem,
Beside the Prince? | Ne razglyazhu!

MEN

Oh, he's an odd one, | Chudak pritvornyi,
A misanthrope and somewhat mad. | Pechal'nyi, strashnyi sumasbrod . . .
He's been abroad, we hear, | V chuzhikh krayakh on byl . . .
But now he's back again; his name's | I vot vernulsya k nam teper' Onegin.
   Onegin.

TATYANA

Yevgeny? | Evgenii?

MEN

Do you know him, then? | On izvesten vam?

TATYANA

We met each other long ago. | Sosed on po derevne nam.
(aside) | O bozhe, pomogi mne skryt'
Oh, heaven! Let me not betray | Dushi uzhasnoe volnen'e . . .
That I am trembling with emotion! |

ONEGIN
(to Gremin)

I seem to know that lady there, | Skazhi mne, knyaz', ne znaesh' ty,
The one who's in the crimson turban; | Kto tam, v malinovom berete,
The Spanish envoy's at her side. | S poslom ispanskim govorit?

GREMIN

Aha! It seems that you're a stranger. | Aha, davno zh ty ne byl v svete!
You must be introduced to her. | Postoi, tebya predstavlyu ya.

ONEGIN

Who is she, though? | Da kto zh ona?

GREMIN

My wife, of course! | Zhena moya!

ONEGIN

I never knew that you were married. | Tak ty zhenat? Ne znal ya rane.
Since when, pray? | Davno li?

	GREMIN
Just about two years.	Okolo dvukh let.
	ONEGIN
To whom?	Na kom?
	GREMIN
The Larin girl, Tatyana.	Na Larinoi, Tat'yane.*
You must have met.	Ty ei znakom?
	ONEGIN
Yes, we were neighbours.	Ya im sosed!

No. 20a Aria.

GREMIN
(dignified and calm, but with warmth)

The gift of love is rightly treasured;	[30] Lyubvi vse vosrasty pokorny,
Its countless blessings can't be measured.	Eyo poryvy blagotvorny
It brings its warming potency	I yunoshe v rastsvete let,
To callow youths when hearts are free;	Edva uvidevshemu svet,
Or to the warrior, old and grey,	I zakalyonnomu sud'boi
Whom fate has tempered in the fray.	Boitsu s sedoyu golovoi!
Onegin, why should I conceal it?	Onegin, ya skryvat' ne stanu:
I'm so in love, I must reveal it.	Bezumno ya lyublyu Tat'yanu!
A wasted, melancholy life	Tosklivo zhizn' moya tekla,
Is what I led until my wife	Ona yavilas'i dala,
Like sun at last on darkest ocean	Kak solntsa luch sredi nenast'ya,
Awoke my heart to new emotion.	Mne zhizn' i molodost', i schast'e!
Amid this turmoil and dissension,	Sredi lukavykh, malodushnykh,
This world of ignorance and hate,	Shal'nykh, balovanykh detei,
Where hypocrites can win attention	Zlodeev i smeshnykh i skuchnykh,
And cowards patronise and prate;	Tupykh, privyazchivykh sudei;
Among coquettes who swear devotion	Sredi koketok bogomol'nykh,
And fawning fops who court promotion,	Sredi kholop'ev dobrovol'nykh,
Amid morality's decay	Sredi vsednevnykh modnykh stsen,
And friends who'd cheat you and betray;	Uchtivykh, laskovykh izmen,
In all our hollow show of fashion,	Sredi kholodnykh prigorov
This endless, futile, social round	Zhestokoserdnoi suety,
Where scarce an honest man is found	Sredi dosadnoi pustoty
Who'll keep his word or show compassion,	Raschotov, dum i razgovorov,
Tatyana's virtue seemed to shine	Ona blistaet, kak zvezda
With pure devotion, long denied me,	Vo mrake nochi, v nebe chistom,
As if some power that was divine	I mne yavlyaetsya vsegda
Had sent an angel down to guide me.	V siyan'e angela luchistom! . . .

No. 21 Scene and Arioso.

And now, you must be introduced to her.	I tak, poidyom, tebya predstavlyu ya!

Prince Gremin leads Onegin over to Tatyana.

My dear, allow me to present you	[10] Moi drug, pozvol' tebe predstavit'
To my good friend and relative, Onegin.	Rodnyu i druga moevo, Onegina!

Onegin bows deeply. Tatyana returns his greeting with utter simplicity, as if in no way embarrassed.

TATYANA

I'm pleased to meet you;	Ya ochen' rada . . .
Indeed I think we've met before.	Vstrechalis' prezhde s vami my!

---

* 'Tat'yane' is sometimes interjected by Onegin in Russian performances, as it is in Pushkin's poem and Tchaikovsky's autograph libretto.

	ONEGIN
In the country . . . yes . . . we met.	V derevnye . . . da . . . davno.

TATYANA

Do tell me,	Otkuda?
Have you been living there since then?	Uzh ne iz nashikh li storon?

ONEGIN

Oh, no! I've just returned here	O, net! Iz dal'nikh stranstvii
From foreign travels.	Ya vozvratilsya.

TATYANA

When was that?	I davno?

ONEGIN

This morning.	Sevodnya!

TATYANA
(to Gremin)

Dearest, I'm tired now.	[28] Drug moi, ustala ya!

Tatyana leaves on Gremin's arm, returning the greetings of the guests. Onegin follows her with his eyes.

ONEGIN

Is this the very same Tatyana,	Uzhel' ta samaya Tat'yana,
The selfsame timid country girl	Kotoroi ya naedine,
Whose touching innocence and love	V glukhoi, dalyokoi storone,
I once so heartlessly rejected	V blagom pylu nravouchen'ya
With such a moralising lecture?	Chital kogda-to nastavlen'ya?
Yes, she it was, whose youthful passion	Ta devochka, kotoroi ya
I dismissed with such presumption.	Prenebregal v smirennoi dole?
How is it she can now appear	Uzheli to ona byla
So condescending and austere?	Tak ravnodushna, tak smela?
What's wrong with me? I'm in a trance.	No chto so mnoi? Ya kak vo sne!
What is this feeling that has stirred	Chto shevel'nulos' v glubine
My frigid heart to new emotion?	Dushi kholodnoi i lenivoi?
Resentment? Jealousy? Regret?	Dosada? . . . Suetnost? Il' vnov'
Or can it be that I'm in love?	Zabota yunosti — lyubov'?
Yes, there's no doubt at all, I love her,	[11] Uvy, somnen'ya net, — vlyublyon ya!
And all my life will never love another!	Vlyublyon, kak mal'chik, polnyi strasti yunoi:
	Puskai pogibnu ya, no prezhde
It seems I once again recapture	Ya v oslepitel'noi nadezhe
The former joy of youthful rapture.	Vkushu volshebnyi yad zhelanii,
Desire has poisoned me with longing;	Up'yus' nesbytochnoi mechtoi!
Henceforth I'll only think of her.	Vezde, vezde on predo mnoi!
She shall be mine for evermore;	Obraz zhelannyi, dorogoi,
This I shall beg her and implore.	Vezde, vezde on predo mnoyu!
I swear I'll die to win her love once more!	

He rushes out. The Ecossaise begins again.*(see note on p. 86)

Scene Two. *A reception room in Prince Gremin's house.*

No. 22 Final Scene. / Tatyana enters in an elegant morning dress and with a letter in her hand. [30]

TATYANA

Why, why did he return and write this letter?	O, kak mne tyazhelo! Opyat' Onegin
He comes again like some relentless ghost to haunt me!	Stal na puti moyom, kak prizrak besposhchadnyi!
Ah, how that look of his disturbed my peaceful mind,	On vzorom ognennym mne dushu vozmutil!
Stirring the memories of passions left behind!	On strast' zaglokhshuyu tak zhivo voskresil!

89

As long ago now, young and tender-hearted,
He set my loving soul on fire, until we parted.

[1a] Kak budto snova devochkoi ya stala,
Kak budto s nim menya nichto ne razluchalo! . . .

She weeps. Onegin appears at the door. He stands for a moment looking passionately at the weeping Tatyana. Then he hurries to her and falls kneeling at her feet. She looks at him without surprise or anger and then motions him to rise.

I beg you, face me, do not kneel,
For I must speak to you quite plainly.
Onegin, how can you forget that long ago
Our paths were crossed by destiny,
And with what meekness
I heard the lesson that you taught.

Dovol'no, vstan'te! . . . Ya dolzhna
Vam obyasnit'sya otkrovenno.
Onegin, pomnite l' tot chas,

Kogda v sadu, v allee nas
Sud'ba svela, i tak smirenno
Urok vash vyslushala ya?

ONEGIN

Have pity! Show me some compassion.
I was mistaken, and now I'm punished.

[19] O, szhal'tes'! Szhal'tes' nado mnoyu!
Ya tak oshibsya, ya tak nakazan!

Tatyana wipes away her tears and motions Onegin not to interrupt.

TATYANA

Onegin, I was then far younger
And better looking it may be.
I fell in love with you, but tell me
What was your answer to my plea?
You scorned my love with formal coldness
And made me suffer for my boldness.
You said I should be more controlled
And, heavens, how my blood runs cold
When I recall your lack of feeling
And how you lectured me!
Yet you were not to blame.
Now I can realise that you acted quite correctly;
All that you said to me was true.
For *then* you found me far too simple;
Cut off from all this social world
You had no use for me. So tell me,
What makes you tolerate me now?
Perhaps I know why you pursue me
And wrote that fervent letter to me.
I think the reason must be this:
You flatter me because I'm rich
And wife of one who, for his valour,
Lives in the favour of the court.
For what a conquest it would seem
If I should yield to your persuasion!
The world would echo with your fame,
Adding new lustre to your name!

[30] Onegin! Ya togda molozhe.
Ya lushche, kazhetsya, byla
I ya lyubila vas . . . No chto zhe,
Chto v vashem serdtse ya nashla?
Kakoi otvet? Odnu surovost'!

Ne pravda l' — vam byla ne novost'
Smirennoi devochki lyubov'?
I nynche — bozhe! — stynet krov',
Kak tol'ko vspomnyu vzglyad kholodnyi
I etu ispoved'? No vas
Ya ne vinyu! . . . V tot strashnyi chas!
Vy postupili blagorodno,

Vy byli pravy predo mnoi.
Togda — ne pravda li? — v pustyne,
Vdali ot suetnoi molvy,
Ya vam ne nravilas' . . . Chto zh nyne
Menya presleduete vy?
Zachem u vas ya na primete?
Ne potomu l', chto v vysshem svete
Teper' yavlyat'sya ya dolzhna,
Chto ya bogota i znatna,
Chto muzh v srazhen'yakh izuvechen;
Chto nas za to laskaet dvor?
Ne potomu l', chto moi pozor
Teper' by vsemi byl zamechen
I mog by v obshchestve prinest'
Vam soblaznitel'nuyu chest'?

ONEGIN

Ah, Tatyana! Oh, how
Can you believe in such deception
Or think I'd ever stoop so low?
It's clear that you have no conception
Of what I'm willing to forego.
If you but realised how intensely
I feel the agony of love;
How every moment I must stifle
The burning ardour of my heart
Which sets me longing to embrace you
With all the fervour I possess,
To worship you and beg your pardon
For ever causing you distress!

Akh! O bozhe! Uzhel',
Uzhel' v mol'be moei smirennoi
Uvidit vash kholodnyi vzor
Zatei khitrosti prezrennoi?
Menya terzaet vash ukor!
Kogda b vy znali, kak uzhasno
Tomit'sya zhazhdoyu lyubvi,
Terpet' i razumom vsechasno
Smiryat' volnenie v krovi;
Zhelat' obnyat' u vas koleni
I, zarydav, u vashikh nog
Izlit' mol'by, priznan'ya, peni,
Vsyo, vsyo, chto vyrazit' by mog!

90

TATYANA	
I'm weeping!	Ya plachu!
ONEGIN	
Weep, then! Tears from *your* eyes Are precious jewels that I treasure!	Plach'te! Eti slyozy Dorozhe vsekh sokrovishch mira!
TATYANA	
Ah, happiness was once so near us! So near us, so near us!	Akh! Schast'e bylo tak vozmozhno, Tak blizko! Tak blizko!
ONEGIN	
Ah, happiness was once so near us! So near us, so near us!	Akh! Schast'e bylo tak vozmozhno, Tak blizko! Tak blizko!
TATYANA	
Destiny has willed that we should part; There's no returning. I have a husband, so I beg, Yes, I beseech you now to leave me.	No sud'ba moya uzh reshena, I bezvoziratno! Ya vyshla zamuzh. Vy dolzhny, Ya vas proshy, menya ostavit'!
ONEGIN	
To leave you? To leave you? What, must I leave you? No! No, I have only one desire And must remain with you for ever. Those eyes of yours, that lovely smile, These are the visions none can sever. To live without you and yet know How near you are would be to perish. I'd gladly suffer torment for your sake Or even die, yes, die, Tatyana, die! For you are all to me, yes, all I cherish!	Ostavit'? Ostavit'? Kak, vas ostavit'? Net! Net! Pominutno videt' vas, Povsyudu sledovat' za vami, Ulybku ust, dvizhen', vzglyad, Lovit' vlyublyonnymi glazami, Vnimat' vam dolgo, ponimat' Dushoi vsyo vashe sovershenstvo, Pred vami v strastnykh mukahk zamirat' Blednet' i gasnut': vot blazhenstvo, Vot odna mechta moya, odno blazhenstvo!

With growing passion, Onegin again falls on his knees before her and seizes her hand. Somewhat frightened, she withdraws it.

TATYANA	
Onegin, as a man of honour, You will surely grant my wish!	[31] Onegin, v vashem serdtse est' I gordost' i pryamaya chest' . . .
ONEGIN	
No, no, I cannot leave you now!	Ya ne mogu ostavit' vas!
TATYANA	
Yevgeny, I not only ask But beg of you to leave me!	Evgenii, vy dolzhny, Ya vas proshu, menya ostavit'!
ONEGIN	
Have pity!	O, szhal'tes'!
TATYANA	
Then learn the truth, I can't conceal it — Ah, I love you still!	Zachem skryvat', zachem lukavit'! Akh! Ya vas lyublyu! . . .

Tatyana, overwhelmed by her confession, sinks on Onegin's breast. He takes her in his arms but she, recovering her senses quickly, frees herself from his embrace.

ONEGIN	
You love me still! What is this magic you have spoken? What heaven, ecstasy! For *this* is how I knew Tatyana!	Chto slyshu ya? Kakoe slovo ty skazala? O, radnost'! Zhizn' moya! Ty prezhneyu Tat'yanoi stala!
TATYANA	
No, no! Former days cannot return.	Net, net! Proshlovo ne vorotit'!

The die is cast; I have a husband	Ya otdana teper' drugomu!
And mean to keep the vow I swore.	Moya sud'ba uzh reshena,
I shall be his for evermore.	Ya budu vek emu verna!

She tries to leave but sits down, overcome. Onegin kneels down before her, wildly impassioned.

ONEGIN

You have confessed that you still love me	O, ne goni! Menya ty lyubish',
So I'm resolved in my design.	I ne ostavlyu ya tebya;
Why waste your days in loveless duty?	Ty zhizn' svoyu naprasno sgubish' . . .
Fate has declared that you are mine.	To volya neba: ty moya!
We were intended for each other;	Vsya zhizn' tvoya byla zalogom
Our lives were guided from on high,	Soedineniya so mnoi!
For now I know that God has sent me	I znai: tebe ya poslan bogom,
To guard and love you till I die.	Do groba ya khranitel' tvoi.
Then let the world henceforth discover	Ne mozhesh' ty menya otrinut',
That we belong to one another.	Ty dlya menya dolzhna pokinut'
Forget your home and hear my plea;	Postylyi dom i shumnyi svet,
Ah, leave this place and come with me!	Tebe drugoi dorogi net!

TATYANA
(standing up)

Onegin! Leave me, I entreat you;	[31] Onegin, ya tverda ostanus':
My husband must not find you here.	Sud'boi drugomu ya dana,
I honour and shall never fail him.	S nim budu zhit' i ne rasstanus'.
I mean to keep the vow I gave.	Net, klyatvy pomnit' ya dolzhna!
	(aside)
Although I'm trembling with elation,	Gluboko v serdtse pronikaet
I must not yield to this temptation.	Evo otchayannyi prizyv,
My heart is his, and his alone.	No pyl prestupnyi podaviv,
But duty and honour command me.	Dolg chesti surovyi, svyashchennyi
I'll be true for ever.	Chuvstvo pobezhdaet!

ONEGIN

No,	Net,
For I have sworn I'll not renounce you.	Ne mozhesh' ty menya otrinut'.
In the cause of love all duty must surrender.	Ty dlya menya dolzhna pokinut' vsyo, vsyo!
Forsake your home and come away,	Postylyi dom i shumnyi svet,
For now there is no other way!	Tebe drugoi dorogi net!
Oh, leave your home and come with me.	O, ne goni menya, molyu!
You love me, I know it,	Ty lyubish' menya!
And destiny has shown that you belong	Ty zhizn' svoyu naprasno sgubish'!
To me for evermore!	Ty moya, navek moya!

Onegin tries to draw Tatyana to him; highly overwrought, she struggles to free herself from his embrace but her strength fails her.

TATYANA

Now I must leave you.	Ya udalyayus'!

ONEGIN

No, you must stay!	Net! Net! Net! Net!

TATYANA

Onegin!	Dovol'no!

ONEGIN

Stay, I beg you, do not go!	O, molyu, ne ukhodi!

TATYANA

I'm deaf to all persuasion.	Net, ya tverda ostanus'!

ONEGIN

I love you, I love you!	Lyublyu tebya, lyublyu tebya!

	TATYANA
Don't torture me!	Ostav' menya!
	ONEGIN
I worship you!	Lyublu tebya!
	TATYANA
Farewell for ever!	Proshchai naveki!
	ONEGIN
You are mine!	Ti moya!

Tatyana leaves the room. He stands for a moment, overcome with doubt and despair.

Disgraced and shamed;	Pozor! Toska!
Now only death remains!*	O, zhalkii zhrebii moi!

He rushes out.

---

* This English text is a free version in keeping with the spirit of Tchaikovsky's music, with a half-rhyme to recommend it. The Russian literally means 'Disgrace! Anguish! How pitiable is my fate!'

The final lines caused Tchaikovsky much anxiety before and after the opera was finished. The libretto has the last verse 'O death, O death! I go to seek thee out!' marked through in Tchaikovsky's hand and replaced with the text printed above. In the first piano score (March 3, 1878), beneath the notes of Onegin's last phrase there are no words. It is fully possible that this blank was left until a decision had been taken, for Tchaikovsky had written to K.K. Albrecht on February 15, 1878:

> Ask Samarin to read through the libretto carefully. Now, when the score is already prepared, I cannot change anything in the essential course of the action, but I am earnestly asking kind Ivan Vasil'evich [Samarin] to correct everything in the stage directions that seems to him stupid, inappropriate, awkward, etc..
>
> I ask him also to pay particular attention to the last line.
>
> I was required due to musical and theatrical demands to dramatize powerfully the scene of Tatyana's explanation with Onegin. At the end I have it that Tatyana's husband appears and orders Onegin with a gesture to withdraw. It was necessary to me at this point that Onegin say something, and I put into his mouth the following line, "O death! O death! I go to seek thee out!" It seems to me that this is all stupid, that he must say something else, and what I cannot conceive. So then, I am asking Ivan Vasil'evich that he render me an invaluable service and solve this difficulty.

In the piano score there was this stage direction: ('Prince Gremin enters. Tatyana, having seen him, lets out a cry, and falls into his embrace unconscious. The prince makes an authoritative gesture to leave.'), but no final line. In the second edition the present text without the stage direction had been established. In the third, there is the additional rubric, 'Onegin stands for a moment . . .', as above. See pp. 14 and 31. The direction 'Tatyana leaves the room' is in the libretto but not in the scores.

Selective Discography *by Robert Seeley*

Conductor	G. Solti	M. Ermler	J. Levine
Orchestra/Opera House	Royal Opera House, Covent Garden	Bolshoi Theatre	Dresden Opera
Date	1975	1978	1987
Larina	A. Reynolds	T. Tugarinova	–
Tatyana	T. Kubiak	T. Milashkina	M. Freni
Olga	J. Hamari	T. Sinyavskaya	–
Onegin	B. Weikl	Y. Mazurok	T. Allen
Filippyevna	E. Hartle	L. Avdeyeva	–
Lensky	S. Burrows	V. Atlantov	N. Shicoff
Gremin	N. Ghiaurov	E. Nesterenko	–
Triquet	M. Sénéchal	L. Kuznetsov	–
Captain	W. Mason	A. Japridze	–
Zaretsky	R. van Allan	V. Yaroslavstev	–
UK LP Number	Decca SET 596 (3)	–	DG (for mid-1988 release)
UK Tape Number	Decca K57K32 (2)	–	"
UK CD Number	Decca 417 413-2 (2)	Olympia OCD 115 (2)	"
US LP Number	London OSA 13112 (3)	–	"
US Tape Number	–	–	"
US CD Number	London 417 413-2 (2)	–	"

Bibliography

Much of the research on Pushkin has appeared in Russian only, but John Bayley's *Pushkin: a comparative commentary* (Cambridge, 1971) has become a standard work of reference. In addition to his detailed study of the verse-novel, there is a succinct biography which infers parallels between the circumstances of the duel in *Onegin* and Pushkin's death; readers interested in this aspect may like to pursue it in Henri Troyat's biography of Pushkin, available in an abridged English translation (London, 1971) and in W.N. Vickery's *Pushkin: Death of a Poet* (Indiana and London, 1968). The events in Tchaikovsky's life which drew him to *Onegin* as an operatic subject are covered by David Brown in the second volume of his study on the composer, *Tchaikovsky: The Crisis Years 1874-78* (London, 1982), along with a thorough analysis of the work. Also of interest are a recent book on Pushkin by A.D.P. Briggs (London, 1983) and John Warrack's *Tchaikovsky* (London, 1973); *Tchaikovsky: Letters to his family. An autobiography* translated by Galina von Meck with additional annotations by Percy M. Young (London, 1981) contains several letters which cover the genesis of the opera.

Sir Charles Johnston's lively translation of Pushkin's poem in Penguin Classics (London, 1977) preserves a delicate balance between irony and seriousness. More complex, and better able to point out Pushkin's flexibility of tone in an extensive commentary, is Vladimir Nabokov's four-volume edition (London, 1964). There is a third, with its own special insights, by D. Chizhevsky (Harvard, 1953).

For readers of Russian the following selection made by R.J. Wiley will be of interest: Asaf'ev, Boris Vladimirovich. *Izbrannye trudy* [Selected works]. 5 vols. Moscow, 1952-7. (Volume II contains a reprint of his celebrated study of *Evgenii Onegin*.) Kassin, Evgenii Pavlovich, Semen Stepanovich Geichenko and Grigorii Denisovich Rastorguev. *Priyut, siyan'em muz odetyi* [A Refuge Clothed in the Radiance of the Muses]. Second edition. Moscow, 1982. (An excellent photographic study of the environs where Pushkin lived, embellished with selections from his works.) Krasinskaya, Lia Ammanuilovna. *Opernaya melodika P.I. Chaikovskogo; k vopruso o vzaimodeistvii melodii i rechevoi intonatsii* [The Operatic Melody of P.I. Tchaikovsky; on the Question of the Interaction of Melody and Speech Intonation]. Leningrad, 1986. Protopopov, Vladimir Vasil'evich, and Nadezhda Vasil'evna Tumanina, *Opernoe tvorchestvo Chaikovskogo* [The Operatic Works of Tchaikovsky]. Moscow, 1957. Rozanova, Yuliya Adreevna. *Istoriya russkoi muzyki, Tom II; Vtoraya polovina XIX veka; Kniga tret'ya; P.I. Chaikovskii* [The History of Russian Music, Volume II; Second Half of the XIX Century; Book Three; P.I. Tchaikovsky]. Moscow, 1981. Sin'kovskaya, Natal'ya Nikolaevna. *O garmonii P.I. Chaikovskogo* [About P.I. Tchaikovsky's Harmony]. Moscow, 1983. Tumanina, Nadezhda Vasil'evna. *Chaikovskii; put' k masterstvu 1840-1977* [Tchaikovsky; the Path to Mastery 1840-1877]. Moscow, 1962. Tsukkerman, Viktor Abramovich. *Vyrazitel'nye sredstva liriki Chaikovskogo* [The Expressive Means of Tchaikovsky's Lyricism]. Moscow, 1971.

Contributors

Caryl Emerson is Professor of Slavic Languages and Literatures at Princeton University and the author of *Boris Godunov: transpositions of a Russian theme*.

Roland John Wiley is a professor of musicology at the University of Michigan at Ann Arbor and the author of *Tchaikovsky's Ballets* (Oxford).

Natalia Challis is a Lecturer in Russian at the Department of Slavic Languages and Literatures at the University of Michigan at Ann Arbor, and has recently completed a book on Rachmaninoff and his songs.

David Lloyd-Jones is Artistic Director of Opera North and formerly Assistant Music Director at ENO. A specialist in Russian opera, his translation of *Boris Godunov* is in Opera Guide 11 and his edition of the original version of that score is published by Oxford, and by Muzyka, the State Publishing House of the U.S.S.R. He has also translated *The Queen of Spades* and *Francesca da Rimini*.

Urszula Koszut as Tatyana and Claudio Nicolai as Onegin at the Cologne Opera, production by Hans Neugebauer, designed by Andreas Majewski and Jan Skalicky, 1983 (photo: Paul Leclaire)